SANTA ANA PUBLIC LIBRARY

D0498002

SACRED SITES
OF THE
KNIGHTS
TEMPLAR

SACRED SITES
OF THE
KNIGHTS
TEMPLAR

ANCIENT ASTRONOMERS
AND FREEMASONS AT
STONEHENGE, RENNES-LE-CHATEAU,
AND SANTIAGO DE COMPOSTELA

JOHN K. YOUNG, PH.D.

FAIR WINDS
PRESS
GLOUCESTER, MASSACHUSETTS

First published in the USA in 2003 by
Fair Winds Press
33 Commercial Street
Gloucester, MA 01930

Library of Congress Cataloging-in-Publication Data available

ISBN 1-59233-017-7

10 9 8 7 6 5 4 3 2

Cover design by Mary Ann Smith
Book design by *tabula rasa* graphic design

Printed and bound in Canada

This book is dedicated to the lights of my life,
my wife Paula and my sons Michael and Matthew.

TABLE OF CONTENTS

INTRODUCTION

ALL ACROSS THE CONTINENT OF EUROPE, MASSIVE STONE monuments erected by a prehistoric culture can be found. These megalithic stones, resisting centuries of weathering and assaults by modern men, are all that remain of a society that has been erased by time. Stonehenge is the most familiar of these megalithic monuments, but in fact represents only one of many similar sites. Who were the people who built these monuments? Why were these stones significant to them?

A careful analysis of these sites has revealed that many stones were carefully positioned to point toward the setting sun or moon at specific times of the year. This, perhaps, should not surprise us: What other natural phenomena could be more important and worthy of recording than the positions of the sun, the source of life-giving light and heat that governs the seasons and the harvests that sustain human life? If these monuments were an expression of a religious belief or a quest for the meaning of life, it would only make sense to mark out the yearly cycle of solar and lunar events, which seem to provide a comforting sense of continuity and predictability over the centuries. By observing regular changes in the night sky, people of all times can find a place for their own lives within the cosmos.

The sacred nature of these megalithic sites seems self-evident to any visitor.

What is not quite so obvious is the fact that the most prominent megalithic sites were deliberately located at specific places that are dictated by astronomy. In the following pages, I will show that, in addition to Stonehenge, other megalithic sites in Denmark, England, France, Germany, Ireland, and Spain are all located precisely at specific latitudes that are required to observe particular orientations of the sun and moon at specific times of the year. You will better understand how these sacred sites are reflections of an ancient philosophical system that covered all of Europe.

In addition, you will see that a reverence for the astronomical meaning of these sites did not die out during prehistory, but was preserved secretly into modern times. More modern structures erected at these megalithic sites, including those constructed by the enigmatic order of medieval knights, the Knights Templar, show a continuing interest in astronomy. This interest can partly explain the puzzling and mysterious features found at places like Rennes-le-Chateau in France and Santiago de Compostela in Spain, which have attracted so much interest in recent years. An in-depth appreciation of hidden astronomical themes shines a new light upon the social and religious history of Europe. This book will introduce you to the path I have followed over the last five years and, one by one, will show you the clues that have led to the discovery of these hidden aspects of European history.

✳

CHAPTER 1

Megalithic Sites Around Stonehenge

PERHAPS THE MOST FAMOUS MEGALITHIC MONUMENT IN THE world is Stonehenge, located in the county of Wiltshire in south central England. Stonehenge is familiar to all of us, and yet it retains an air of mystery. Why was it built? Who built it, and what is the meaning of its complex pattern of standing stones? Many investigators have struggled throughout the centuries to explain it.

The physical details of Stonehenge have been established with great precision: The positions of each stone have been carefully surveyed and mapped, and the age of the monument has been estimated by radiocarbon dating of associated organic remains. We now know that Stonehenge dates from about 3000 B.C., making it as old as the pyramids. We also know the precise arrangement of the megalithic stones that compose it. The largest stones at Stonehenge have long been called "Sarsen stones," presumably because early English observers of the monument thought they had been magically erected by foreigners, i.e., Saracens. Some of these large stones are arranged in a horseshoe-shaped profile and stand upright to form three trilithons, a term describing two stone columns capped by a stone lintel. Additional Sarsen stones form a gigantic circle of connected trilithons around the inner horseshoe. Finally, the Sarsen stones are themselves surrounded by a ring of smaller bluestones. These details about Stonehenge nevertheless leave one important question unanswered: Why did ancient peoples go to so much trouble to construct it?

A key to understanding Stonehenge is a knowledge of astronomy. The arrangement of stones at Stonehenge shows a remarkably sophisticated understanding of astronomical events by the ancient peoples of the British Isles who constructed the monument. An American astronomer, Gerald Hawkins, was one of the first to propose a theory that explained a reason for building Stonehenge (Hawkins, 1965). Hawkins became interested in the structure when he learned one long-established fact: The overall axis of the Sarsen stone horseshoe is precisely aligned with the direction of the rising sun on the longest day of the year, the summer solstice. When a smaller stone, the "heel stone," is viewed through the gap in one of the trilithons, the summer solstice sun rises directly above the heel stone (Fig. 1). In addition to these marker stones, an "avenue" bordered by parallel ditches proceeds away from Stonehenge for about a third of a mile in the direction of the rising sun (Hawkins, 1965, p. 50).

Fig. 1

Stone Locations at Stonehenge

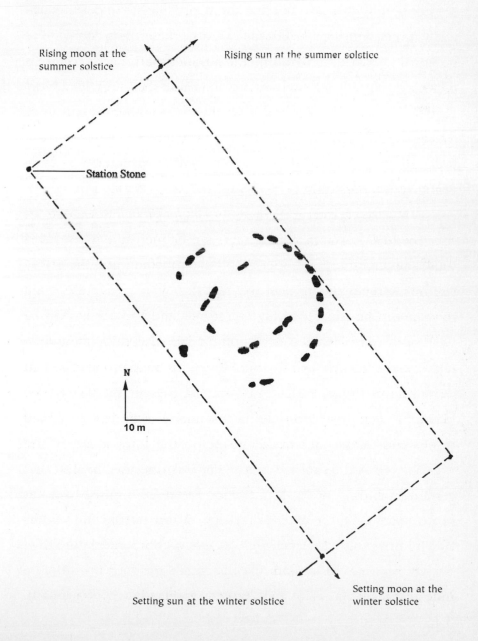

Rising moon at the
summer solstice

Rising sun at the summer solstice

Station Stone

N

10 m

Setting sun at the winter solstice

Setting moon at the
winter solstice

So, some of the stones appear to have been positioned to mark astronomical events.

Positioning stones to point at the sun, while striking, is not actually a very difficult intellectual achievement, since the sun rises at exactly the same location during the summer solstice each year. This will not be true indefinitely, since the axis of the earth "wobbles" very slowly, completing a small circle every 26,000 years. However, for several thousand years, the rising sun will retain the same position within a half of a degree on the horizon (North, 1996; p. 225). Marking out the location of the rising sun, and aligning stones with it, should have been relatively easy for the makers of Stonehenge.

Hawkins, however, found that a much more sophisticated understanding of astronomy was incorporated into the stone alignments. Hawkins used an accurate survey map of Stonehenge to examine positions of standing stones and to compare them with positions of objects in the night sky. This difficult undertaking was accomplished by using a mainframe computer and an astronomical program that was state of the art for the 1960s. Hawkins examined possible astronomical alignments of the stones with large numbers of possible candidates—planets and stars, as well as the sun and moon. He was surprised to find that certain pairs of stones at Stonehenge were also aligned to point to positions of the rising and setting moon during the winter and summer solstices. But why was this such an achievement?

The reason why locating the moon was such a feat is that the moon does not rise and set at the same position each year. Due to

Fig. 2

Full Moon Rise During the Summer Solstice

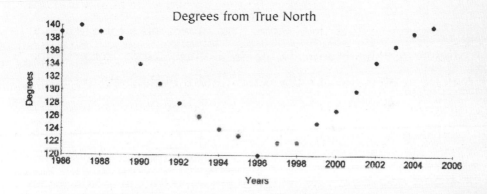

a complex interaction between the orbits of the earth and moon, the full moon during the month of June (June 21 is the actual date of the summer solstice) rises at a slightly different position each year. Over a cycle that repeats every 18.6 years, the rising moon changes its position on the horizon from a maximal 140 degrees away from true north to a minimal 120 degrees away from true north at the latitude of Stonehenge (see Fig. 2). So to mark one of these extreme positions (standstill points) of the full moon at the summer solstice, an observer would have to take measurements for at least nineteen years, and probably for fifty-six years for a more accurate estimate (three cycles of 18.6 years each would bring the moon almost precisely back to its original position, within an interval of 55.8 years). This accomplishment seems remarkable for prehistoric, pre-literate peoples, yet the construction of Stonehenge leaves little doubt that it was achieved.

Why does the moon show such a bizarre cycle of positions throughout the years? We now know that the basic reason is that the sun, moon, and earth are all massive enough and close enough to each other that their fields of gravity continuously interact, pulling and tugging on .the moon and causing the plane of the moon's orbit to wobble. These interactions are so complicated that generations of early astronomers, like Tycho Brahe and Johannes Kepler, despaired of ever being able to precisely predict the position of the moon. It was not until the postulation of gravity by Isaac Newton that a reasonable explanation for the moon's antics was arrived at in 1693. Even the brilliant Newton, however, was unable to create the complex differential equations that would allow predictions of the moon's position that were error free. Newton worked on this problem for over a year and finally abandoned attempts at perfection. It was not until the late eighteenth and nineteenth centuries that the French mathematician, Laplace, and the American astronomer, Hill, were finally able to devise the mathematics that would accurately predict the moon's position (Peterson, 1993, p. 130). So the ability of ancient peoples to mark the positions of the moon at the summer or winter solstices was indeed quite a feat.

Curiously, there are a number of shallow pits, now filled in, that are distributed in a circle around Stonehenge. These pits, called Aubrey holes after their discoverer, are equally spaced and equal fifty-six in number. Hawkins believed that the function of these holes was to keep track of how far along the moon was in time over its 55.8 year tri-cycle of jumps in position. By placing a rock in a pit every year, an observer would know how long to wait before the cycle repeated.

How, then, was the position of the moon indicated at Stonehenge? Not, as it turns out, by any of the main bluestones or Sarsen stones, but actually by the positions of four "station stones" located at the corners of a rectangle staked out around the margins of the main circular monument (see Fig. 1). A person sighting along two of these stones during the right time of the 18.6-year cycle could see the maximal displacement from true north of the setting and rising moon at the winter and summer solstices.

To get an idea of what this could involve, I tried to place the positions of the sun and moon at the summer solstice last year. This is not as easy as you might think. For one thing, ask yourself when you last observed the sun just touching the horizon. Unless you go to the beach frequently, this will not be often, primarily because the horizon is not actually visible to most of us. We either tend to live in cities, or else in hilly or heavily forested regions that obscure a vision of the horizon. I was able to overcome this obstacle by walking over to a flat parking garage close to my house. The roof was high enough so that I could see the horizon.

The next step in amateur astronomy is to consult the newspaper, which helpfully lists the times of sunrise, moonset, and so on, on any given day (this wouldn't have been available to the Stonehenge builders!). In this way it is easy to make a chalk mark on a wall, step back twenty paces or so, and wait for sunset to make another chalk mark on the pavement that marks the direction of the setting sun. Determining the direction of moonset is similar, if not quite so obvious as sunset: The moon can set in almost any direction in the sky and at almost any time of the day, quite unlike the sun (check your own newspaper listing if you don't believe me!). So, on the night of the summer solstice, at 2:30 A.M., I went back to the garage to mark the position of the setting moon (avoiding the strange looks of a few people who were picking up their cars in the middle of the night). I found, to my chagrin, that rain clouds obscured that region of the sky and hid the moon! I had to wait an entire year to look at the moon again. This gave me a real appreciation of how persistent the builders of Stonehenge must have been to gather the information they needed.

The long periods of time required to make astronomical observations is actually confirmed by detailed archeological excavations at Stonehenge. The version of Stonehenge we now see is not the first one; it was preceded over several hundred years by somewhat less complicated versions on the same site that used wooden poles or smaller stones as markers. The Stonehenge we know represents the culmination of many years of observations, reverence, and effort.

Once the astronomical data had been acquired, the actual construction of the final version of Stonehenge must have required a lot of persistence and energy. Some of the larger Sarsen stones have been estimated to weigh as much as fifty tons; they were probably quarried about twenty miles away and dragged to the site. The smaller bluestones (eighty-two in number) weigh about five tons each; the only site of origin for this type of stone in the British Isles has been determined to be in Wales. This means that these heavy stones were transported by raft or sledges for some 240 miles! Why go to so much trouble? Why drag these stones to this specific site? Couldn't Stonehenge have been constructed at a site closer to the desired stones? What is so special about the location of Stonehenge (Fig. 3)?

Fig. 3

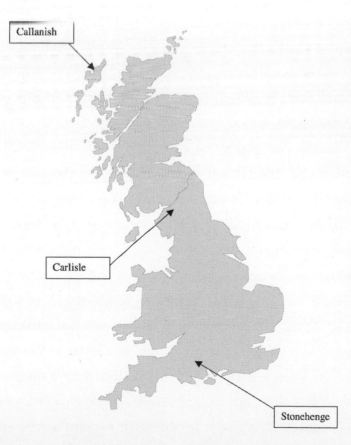

For one thing, as I noted above, it is essential to actually see the horizon from an astronomical observatory. The flat Salisbury plain of the Stonehenge locale does provide this ability. But there is more to it than that.

As noted in Fig. 1, the maximal standstill points of the rising moon at the solstices can be sighted along one edge of a rectangle marked out by station stones, and the setting and rising sun at the solstices can be seen along other edges of the rectangle. In other words, the sun-moon angles amount to almost exactly 90 degrees at Stonehenge. As Hawkins noted, if the location of Stonehenge had been just thirty miles further north, these exact angles would not have been possible. The only conclusion is that the specific site for Stonehenge was deliberately chosen so that the sun-moon angles would describe a perfect rectangle. Imagine the time and effort needed to measure the sun-moon angles throughout the British Isles and to finally determine the perfect site to celebrate these astronomical events! This resulted in Stonehenge being constructed at precisely the latitude of 51.1 degrees north of the equator, and nowhere else.

What is so special about a 90-degree angle between the positions of the sun and moon? Since the Stonehenge builders left no written records, it is basically impossible to know what their culture or system of religious values was like, or why such an angle might have been significant for them. However, some qualities of a 90-degree angle are obvious: Ninety degrees divides a circle into four equal parts, just as a year can be divided into four seasons; a

90-degree angle can be used to construct squares or rectangles, right triangles (like an equilateral triangle), or a 30-60-90 degree triangle (in which the hypotenuse is exactly twice as long as one of the sides), and so on. It is not too difficult to imagine how a 90-degree separation between the sun and the moon, placing the influences of the rulers of day and night in opposition and in balance with each other, could have a mystic or symbolic significance. The importance of astronomical alignment in dictating the geographical location of a ceremonial site is a major theme that I want to emphasize throughout this book.

Although Stonehenge is the most prominent megalithic structure in the area, it in fact is only a portion of a larger, extraordinary complex of structures in Wiltshire. One massive megalithic construction about twenty miles north of Stonehenge is on a site named Avebury, a more modern village that partially covers a huge collection of stones placed in prehistoric times. The stones, jutting 9-19 feet out of the ground, are placed around a huge circular ditch one thousand feet in diameter that was originally twenty-five feet deep and encircled by a bank of earth eighteen feet high. One huge, square stone, called the Swindon stone after the nearest city, is nineteen feet high and weighs an estimated sixty-five tons. This colossal construction is one of the largest in the British Isles, and also underscores the likelihood that ancient peoples particularly venerated the location of Stonehenge and were willing to make an extraordinary effort to express their feelings about it.

The immediate environments of both Stonehenge and Avebury are rural and not densely populated. Since few traces of habitation from more modern times persist at these sites, it is difficult to know how long people continued to venerate this region of Wiltshire. It is of interest to us, in the context of the overall theme of this book, that near Avebury, in the town of Marlborough, the remains of a stone structure belonging to the Knights Templar (Temple Rockley) can be seen (Howarth, 1982, p. 237). We will discuss numerous connections between megalithic sites dedicated to astronomy and the Knights Templar throughout this book.

Does astronomy similarly influence the construction of any other megalithic sites in the British Isles? Hawkins describes another site, Callanish, located on an island called Lewis in the Outer Hebrides Islands (Fig. 3). This is a circle of thirteen stones with several straight rows of stones associated with it. Many of these stones are aligned to point at the setting solsticial sun or to the extreme positions of the setting moon, just as at Stonehenge; however, unlike at Stonehenge, the sun–moon angles are *not* perpendicular to each other at this latitude. The latitude at which Callanish was constructed may nevertheless have its own significance: It is close to the "arctic circle" for the moon, and once every 18.6 years, the rising moon barely climbs above the horizon and appears between a gap in the surrounding mountains before setting again at this specific locale. This could be sheer coincidence, but it is more likely that this megalithic structure was also deliberately constructed at a site dictated by astronomy.

Hundreds of other megalithic sites exist in the British Isles, and it appears that many of them also have some connection to astronomical observations. A wonderful recent book by John North (North, 1996) discusses the astronomical context of many of these sites, including Stonehenge, in considerable technical detail. One site of particular interest is the so-called "Long Man," an outline of a human figure cut into the side of a hill near Wilmington in East Sussex. The creators of this figure cut a trench into the green turf to expose the underlying white chalk, thereby drawing an outline of a man holding two upright staffs, one in each outstretched hand. The figure is about 270 feet long and can be seen for a considerable distance from the hillside (see also Sykes, 1993, and Westwood, 1987).

The meaning of this striking figure has long been unclear. North, however, demonstrates quite convincingly that the shape and orientation of the Long Man very closely matches the appearance of the human figure in the constellation of Orion, which regularly sets on the horizon just above the Long Man. In our current era, Orion no longer sets in perfect alignment with the horizon of the Long Man; however, a computer-generated estimate of the setting of Orion in 3400 B.C. does align perfectly with the figure. So this may be another ancient site that was created to celebrate an astronomical event. Of all these megalithic sites, however, none is as elaborate, or required as much skill and effort to build, as Stonehenge. It seems clear that the specific astronomical significance of the location of Stonehenge made it the foremost site in the British Isles.

As we shall see, Stonehenge is not the only site in Europe dedicated to astronomy and located in accord with astronomical principles. I intend to show how other sites—Aachen in Germany, Rennes-le-Chateau in France, and Santiago de Compostela in Spain—are also located at astronomically significant latitudes.

Fig. 4

Sacred Megalithic Sites are Found at Specific Latitudes

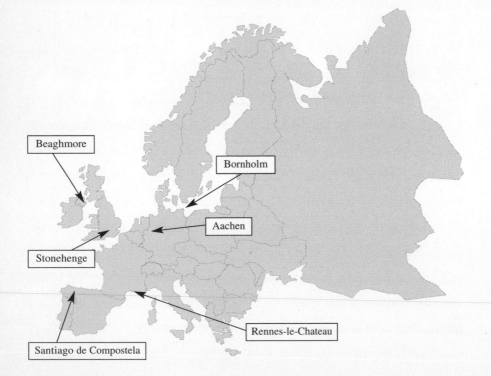

Fig. 4. Sacred megalithic sites are found at specific latitudes: A = beaghmore, b = Bornholm, C = Stonehenge, d = Aachen, E = Santiago de Compostela, f = rennes-le-Chateau

✳

CHAPTER 2

Sacred Sites Outside of the British Isles

THE PREVIOUS CHAPTER DEMONSTRATED THAT MEGALITHIC monuments at Stonehenge and Callanish were not constructed at random locations in the British Isles, but were located at sites required for specific astronomical observations possible only at certain latitudes. But what about megalithic sites in other locations? Can astronomy be used to explain these as well?

The astronomical orientations of many other prehistoric structures have become recognized over the last twenty years (Krupp, 1994). But the astronomical basis for the *locations* of these structures has not been fully recognized. By utilizing astronomical principles in this detective story, I will try to summarize the data showing that many structures—in Europe and even in ancient Egypt—were constructed in ancient times at latitudes dictated by astronomy. Furthermore, it is clear that the astronomical meaning of these sacred sites was not forgotten, but was preserved secretly. Clues revealing this knowledge can be found in the structural details and geographical alignments of cathedrals and castles constructed by the Church and the Knights Templar.

Egypt

Some of the most dramatic examples of ancient monuments related to astronomy are in Egypt. Recently, the oldest known megalithic stone circle was discovered in the Nabta Playa region of southern Egypt, located west of the famous temple at Abu-Simbel. This site consists of a circle of stones associated with five rows of standing and toppled megaliths. Some of the rows are oriented due south or east, and some are oriented to point in the direction of the setting summer solstice sun. The whole complex is at least 6000 years old. Nabta Playa is located at a latitude of 22.5 degrees, just south of the Tropic of Cancer, a latitude of great astronomical significance. At the latitude of the Tropic of Cancer, the noonday midsummer sun shines directly overhead, so that no shadows are cast in any direction. It is very likely that the placement of this monument at this specific location is not coincidental; many pre-industrial cultures in this region of the world are known to have been knowledgeable about this eerie midsummer event (Malville, 1998). This site marks the first known attempt of the ancient Egyptian culture to create astronomically-oriented objects. Other later Egyptian monuments reveal that this early interest in astronomical objects continued and became more sophisticated.

The complex of the Sphinx and the pyramids at Giza themselves reveal astronomical and geodetic orientations that are not
commonly appreciated, and have been discussed in fascinating
books by Graham Hancock (Hancock, 1996) and Peter Tompkins
(Tompkins, 1971). The eastern side of the pyramid of Cheops is
oriented to true north with incredible precision: within 3 arc
minutes (5% of a single degree) of true north (Hancock, 1996, p.
41). Also, the latitude of the pyramids is curious: 29 degrees, 58
minutes, 51 seconds north of the equator, i.e., about a mile from
the 30th parallel of latitude, which is exactly one-third of the
distance from the equator to the north pole. This almost suggests
that the Egyptians placed the pyramids at a position on the globe
defined by a simple geometrical point. The Greek word *geometry*,
after all, arises from the phrase "to measure the earth." Is it possible
that ancient Egyptians knew that the earth was round, accurately
estimated its diameter, and positioned the pyramids one-third of
the distance to the pole? Or is the location of the pyramids close
to 30 degrees north mere coincidence?

The man who is generally credited with the first accurate
determination of the earth's diameter is the Greek philosopher
Eratosthenes of Alexandria (Egypt), who, in about 220 B.C., was
curious as to why the sun shone directly overhead and cast no
shadows on the day of the summer solstice in Aswan, a region
in southern Egypt. However, in Alexandria, on the same day,
the sun was not precisely overhead and cast a small shadow
showing that it was displaced from the exact zenith by 1/50th

of the circumference of the heavens. How would this have helped Eratosthenes measure the earth?

To understand this, a little review of the positioning of the earth relative to the sun is in order (Fig. 5). If the axis of rotation of the earth, passing through the north and south poles, were exactly perpendicular to the earth's orbit around the sun, it would be much easier to visualize and understand the positioning of the sun in the sky. In such a situation, a person living at the equator would see the sun rise due east, pass overhead until reaching a zenith exactly 90 degrees from the horizon, and then descend until setting due west. This would happen every day of the year, and there would be no seasons. A person located at the north or south poles would never see the sun rising above the horizon. A person located 20 degrees of latitude north of the equator would see the sun rise, but it would reach a point in the sky 20 degrees short of being directly overhead, and then it would set.

Needless to say, this does not happen, because the earth's axis of rotation is tilted about 23.5 degrees away from the plane of earth's orbit. Thus, during the winter, the Northern Hemisphere is tilted away from the direct rays of the sun, and becomes colder. As the earth moves around its orbit, the Northern Hemisphere "turns its face" more directly toward the sun, and receives a maximal amount of sunlight on June 21, the summer solstice. Because of this, a person located at the latitude of 23.5 degrees, rather than at the equator, will see the sun standing directly overhead on the day of the summer solstice. It turns out that Aswan is located very

Fig. 5

The Tilt of the Earth's Axis in Relation to the Seasons

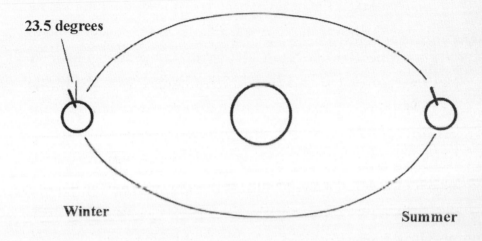

23.5 degrees

Winter

Summer

close to this latitude of 23.5 degrees. Knowing this, Eratosthenes then paid a number of men to accurately pace off the distance between Aswan and Alexandria, which turned out to be about 489 miles. Eratosthenes reasoned that this distance must represent 1/50th of the circumference of the earth. By multiplying 489 miles by 50, Eratosthenes arrived at estimates of the earth's circumference and diameter that are surprisingly close to modern estimates (Hawkins, 1983, p. 151).

It seems clear from this account that the concept that the earth is a sphere was already known in Egypt before the time of Eratosthenes. But did Eratosthenes himself discover the earth's diameter, or did he merely reconfirm information that had long been known in Egypt before his time? No current information is available about the latter possibility, but if it proves true, it might explain the location of the pyramids of Giza.

Another hint of Egyptian knowledge of astronomy and the tilt of the earth's axis might be derivable from an examination of another Egyptian structure, the temple on the west bank of the Nile in southern Egypt at Abu-Simbel. This temple is the largest of its type ever to be cut from solid rock and is faced with four colossal, seated stone statues of Rameses II carved out of the cliff face. It is located just south of the Tropic of Cancer, e.g. at the latitude of 22.1 degrees. The positioning of this temple is more than one degree south of 23.5 degrees, so it would not be located precisely underneath the zenith of the sun at the summer solstice. On the other hand, Aswan, which was selected by Eratosthenes as the site that underlies the zenith of the sun, is also not precisely located at the Tropic of Cancer, and is almost one degree to the north out of position. Perhaps the knowledge of the exact site of the Tropic of Cancer was inexact in ancient Egypt, and the siting of the temple at Abu-Simbel reflects this. Or, even more likely, the site on the banks of the Nile precisely at the latitude of the Tropic of Cancer was not suitable for large-scale construction.

This temple is no longer at its original position, because the rising waters of Lake Nasser, trapped by the construction of the Aswan High Dam in the 1960s, required that the temple be cut into massive blocks and reassembled on a bluff safely above the water. Before the temple was relocated, however, an interesting astronomical phenomenon was observable within it. The temple contains a long hallway that leads 200 feet into the darkness of the sandstone. Every year, on October 17, a shaft of sunlight passed down through this hallway and briefly illuminated statues of the sun god Re-Hor-Akhety, Rameses II, and Amon-Re, the god of upper Egypt. Hawkins investigated the site in the 1980s and speculated that the date of October 17 might have been of considerable significance to Egypt: It roughly marks the time when the Nile declines from its peak flooding stage. Next to the main temple is a smaller chapel dedicated to the sun god. The axis of this chapel is oriented to point precisely at sunrise during the winter solstice (Hawkins, 1983, p. 123; Krupp, 1984, p. 317).

Incidentally, some other aspects of astronomy and geometry might also trace their origin to Egyptian thinking. Why, for example, do we divide a circle (and the night sky) into 360 divisions called degrees? Why not divide a circle into twenty, fifty, or a hundred parts? While the origin of this convention appears lost in the mists of time, it might be traceable to the Egyptian calendar. Ancient Egyptians divided the year into twelve months of thirty days each, for a total "year" amounting to 360 days—the remaining five extra days were considered "off the books" for that year (North, 1996, p. 301). Perhaps this division of celestial time carried over into a general system for dividing up a circle. A similar astronomical and calendar scheme was employed by the ancient Babylonians.

Other details about the structure of the Great Pyramid of Cheops reveal more astronomical alignments. Two large chambers— now called the Queen's Chamber and the King's Chamber—were constructed deep within the interior of this pyramid. From each chamber, two long, narrow, hollow shafts were constructed between the stones that lead upward and away from the chambers (Hancock, 1983, p. 57). The two shafts leading from the King's Chamber eventually penetrate the outer layer of stones of the pyramid to reach the outside; for a long time, these were thought to be ventilation shafts. However, the shafts leading from the Queen's Chamber do *not* reach the outside world, stopping just short of the surface of the pyramid, even though they still point accurately to specific stars. This calls into question the function of these laboriously constructed, and extremely straight, hollow shafts. What was their purpose?

Both sets of shafts, once again, point accurately in the north-south direction. This direction is the axis of rotation of the night sky: A given constellation achieves its maximal elevation from the horizon as it appears to rotate around the pole star. When the night sky of 2500 B.C. is modeled using a computer program, the maximal elevation of any constellation at the location of Giza is easily determined. As it turns out, these shafts from the pyramid accurately point to the maximal elevations of significant stars. One star is the brightest star in the "belt" of the constellation Orion, which the Egyptians identified with Osiris, a prominent, sacred figure in Egyptian mythology and religion. Another shaft points at Sirius, associated with the goddess Isis. Another star was alpha Draconis, which at that time was the pole star (in our era, Polaris is now the pole star, due to the slow "wobble" of earth's axis of rotation over 26,000 years, which causes it to point at different stars over time). The fourth star was in the constellation of the Little Bear (Little Dipper). It thus seems that these shafts were designed as mystic avenues of communication between the interior of the Pyramid and stars in the night sky.

Incidentally, it's also interesting to note that the people who originally discovered these shafts in the pyramid were Freemasons. The Queen's Chamber shafts were discovered in 1872 by an English engineer and Freemason, Waynman Dixon. He and his brother John traveled to Egypt in that year, inspired by both a fascination for ancient Egypt and by the legends and allegories of Freemasonry, which stated that arcane secrets of geometry and astronomy originated in Egypt and in the Temple of Jerusalem at the legendary dawn of Freemasonry. Later on, these same brothers were commissioned by wealthy and influential Masons, Sir James Alexander and Sir Erasmus Wilson, to supervise the transfer of a 200-ton obelisk, dating from the reign of Thutmosis III, to London, where it stands today (Hancock, 1983, p. 57).

The pyramids of Giza in Egypt are just one example of a preoccupation with orienting structures in astronomically significant ways. Another example is the magnificent Temple of Amon-Re at Karnak, in southern Egypt. This temple contains twelve huge stone columns, each eighty feet tall, that contribute to a long axis of the temple that measures 1860 feet. This axis points to the rising of the sun at the winter solstice (in 1483

B.C., the year of construction) with an accuracy within 1/10th of one degree (Hawkins, 1983, p. 126; Krupp, 1984, p. 312).

What do all these astronomical inclinations of the ancient Egyptians have to do with sacred sites in Europe? There is not necessarily any direct connection between the ancient cultures of Egypt and Europe. However, it seems likely that the older civilization of Egypt did have some influence upon the ideas, outlook, and culture of younger European civilizations bordering the Mediterranean. Egyptian notions about astronomy, geometry, mathematics, and architecture do seem to have influenced their counterparts in, for example, ancient Greece. For instance, it is known that as early as 600 B.C., the Greek (Athenian) statesman Solon visited Egypt, toured its temples, and tried to gain some understanding of Egyptian history and ancient wisdom (Clayton, 1994, p. 9). As a matter of fact, a controversial scholastic treatment of this subject by the historian Martin Bermal (Bermal, 1991) suggests that a great deal of the culture and philosophy of ancient Greece are in fact directly derived from Egypt. For example, Bermal notes that a major topic in the writings of the Greek historian, Herodotus, around 450 B.C., was the immigration of people from Egypt to Greece hundreds of years earlier (Bermal, 1991, p. 98). While a flurry of critical reaction to this book suggests that Bermal might have overstated his case somewhat, the overall gist of his argument does appear to have some validity. It is not unreasonable to propose some commonality of thinking between ancient Egypt and close-by European communities. Of course, there is no reason to believe that these communities could not have developed some or all of their orientation toward astronomical topics independently of other cultures.

France

Is there, then, any evidence for ceremonial sites in Europe that have some of the same astronomical orientations as those seen at Stonehenge or in Egypt? Hundreds of megalithic sites throughout Europe have characteristics similar to those in the British Isles and suggest a broad commonality of religious/ceremonial thinking throughout Europe, just as common Christian themes spread throughout Europe several thousand years later. Curiously, one of these ancient sites is now the location of a great medieval cathedral at Chartres, just southwest of Paris.

Originally, at this location, a so-called dolmen of large stones supporting a flat "roof" stone was constructed by megalithic builders (Westwood, 1996, p. 20). Nearby, a well surrounded by a mound was also created. Later, these structures became venerated by Celtic priests, who established a cult of a virgin, who was represented by a carved, wooden image. Later, in the third century A.D., Christians adopted this image of a virgin and incorporated it into a grotto within a succession of five churches that were built upon this site. All five of these churches were destroyed by fire, but the sixth church, begun in 1194, gradually grew into one of the most magnificent Gothic cathedrals in Europe. This wonderful cathedral still retains some connections with its megalithic origin. For example, at noon on June 21, the summer solstice, a ray of light passes through a unique, clear pane in a stained glass window placed to precisely illuminate a special flagstone set into the floor. Some memory of an astronomical purpose of the original megalithic site must clearly have been retained and preserved in this curious detail.

This is but one of the most dramatic examples of how many medieval churches in Europe were positioned to incorporate and supplant the pre-Christian, mystic attributes of a megalithic site. A generalized effort to either incorporate the remnants of megalithic beliefs into a Christian context or obliterate them altogether is explicitly stated to be Church policy in a number of documents. For example, a letter from Pope Gregory to Abbot Mellitus, cited in the Venerable Bede's *Ecclesiastical History of England,* states that pagan temples should be sanctified and converted to churches. Patrick, Bishop of the Hebrides, directed that a church be built wherever a megalithic stone was found. Similar practices were common in France. So the positioning of churches according to megalithic, astronomical principles should not be regarded as doubtful or even surprising (Brown, 1976, p. 234).

Carnac

Perhaps the most well-known megalithic site in France is at a location named Carnac, in Brittany. At this site, precise rows of hundreds of standing stones positioned over very large areas can

be seen and, in fact, are visited by hundreds of thousands of fasci-
nated tourists each year. This megalithic site has been meticulously
surveyed and studied by Alexander Thom, a Scottish civil engineer
who took an interest in megalithic architecture and who has
published numerous studies that have been very well received by
the scientific community. His findings show a definite interest in
astronomy by the builders of the site.

Thom proposed that at least two lunar observatories can be
discerned from the placement of stones around Carnac. One
observatory centers around a famous stone called Le Grand
Menhir located at a site called Locmariaquer (*menhir* is a Breton
word for standing stone). The Grand Menhir is unfortunately
no longer standing upright—it appears to have toppled some-
time before the seventeenth century. However, when it was
erect, it seems that about nineteen meters of its slender twenty-
two-meter length pointed at the sky. Since its weight has been
estimated at 330 tons, an incredible amount of effort must have
been required to quarry, move, and erect it in a pit in the
ground. The Grand Menhir is the largest single megalithic stone
known in Europe; its size compares favorably with similar
Egyptian obelisks from the Temple of Karnak, e.g. the obelisk
with a height of 19.5 meters erected by Tuthmosis I (Wilkinson,
2000, p. 59). While the Grand Menhir is not as elaborately
carved as the obelisks of Egypt, the feat of creating and moving
it suggests that the society of ancient Brittany shared some of
the abilities of the more advanced culture of Egypt.

Why go to the trouble of carving and erecting such an enormous stone? Thom maintains that the answer relates to astronomy. The Grand Menhir is located on a small peninsula that extends into the Bay of Quiberon. Since it is surrounded on three sides by water, it is ideally situated for observation of the rising and setting of the sun and moon on the horizon. Thom has proposed that the Grand Menhir was used to point at the positions of the moon, not unlike the foresight on the barrel of a rifle. However, if the stone was to function as a foresight, where were the backsights located?

If lines are drawn from the Grand Menhir to three prominent, though smaller, standing stones present in the area, it can be shown that these lines point to positions of the rising or setting moon at the solstices. If a neolithic observer stood behind stones at Le Moustoir and looked at the faraway (nine kilometers distant) needle of the Grand Mehnir, calculations show that the setting full moon at the winter solstice (minimal standstill point) should have appeared at the tip of the Grand Menhir. Other stones at Quiberon and Kerran, when lined up with the tip of the Grand Menhir, point to the positions of the rising full moon at the winter and summer solstices (maximal standstill point) (Wood, 1978, p. 145).

The other lunar observatory identified by Thom centers around a large (six meters tall) standing stone at a site called Le Manio. Five backsight stones located within one-half to one mile from the stone at Le Manio allow the identification of the spots on the horizon for the setting sun at the winter solstice and for the moon at the maximal and minimal standstill points (Wood, 1978, p. 158).

Impressive as these sites are, they are not the only examples of an organized array of megalithic stones in the vicinity of Carnac. Long rows of megalithic stones are carefully positioned at Kermario and Le Menec. At Le Menec there are 1100 megaliths arranged in twelve parallel rows that extend for about one kilometer; the largest stones in this arrangement are four meters tall and weigh as much as fifty tons. Some of the rows of stones point to dolmens, or burial tombs, on hilltops; many others also appear to be aligned to point at the sun and moon, although the astronomical orientations are not as clear or as easy to confirm as the ones associated with the Grand Menhir. One of the earth-covered megalithic tombs in the area, the tumulus St. Michel, actually has an old Christian chapel on its summit (Wood, 1978, p. 140).

Analysis of buried artifacts suggests the builders of Carnac traded with other megalithic centers in Spain and the British Isles. The remains of a small Roman town located about a mile east of Carnac were excavated in 1874. Also, tradition has it that a Templar convent was once located at this spot (*Encyclopedia Brittanica,* vol. 4, 1952 Edition).

These observations are all very interesting, but what about the actual location of Carnac (latitude = 47.6 degrees N, longitude = 3 degrees W)? We know that the latitude of Stonehenge was critical for observing a 90-degree angle between the sun and the moon at the summer solstice, and that astronomical considerations appeared to dictate the precise location of Stonehenge at a latitude of 51.1 degrees. Are any unusual astronomical alignments visible at the latitude of Carnac? How would we go about finding this out?

Hawkins confirmed the astronomical alignments of stones at Stonehenge by comparing the surveyed locations of stones with the computed directions of the sun and moon, using a complex program and a mainframe computer. Fortunately for us, the power of current personal computers and the widespread availability of appropriate software makes Hawkins's task considerably easier now. One excellent program is called SkyMap Pro 4.0, created by JASC Software, Inc., Eden Prairie, Minnesota. This program includes some 10,000 objects from the Saguaro Astronomy Club database that are visible through amateur telescopes, plus an additional 150,000 objects, such as distant galaxies obtained from other databases. The positions of all of these objects can be plotted on a map of the sky adjustable for any latitude and for any time between 4000 B.C. and A.D. 8000. This program allowed me to compute the 18.6-year cycle of the positions of the full moon at the time of the solstice (Fig. 1), and accurately duplicated the moon and sun positions published by Hawkins for the latitude of Stonehenge (Hawkins, 1965, p. 110). The next step was to apply this program to the latitude of Carnac. The results are shown in Table 1:

Table 1

Lunar and Solar Locations on the Horizon at the Maximum Standstill Point at Carnac

Summer Solstice, 2006

Full Moonrise (June 11)	136 degrees from true north
Full Moonset (June 11)	226 degrees
Sunrise (June 21)	54 degrees
Sunset (June 21)	307 degrees

Winter Solstice, 2006

Full Moonrise (Dec. 5)	47 degrees
Full Moonset (Dec. 5)	312 degrees
Sunrise (Dec. 21)	143 degrees
Sunset (Dec. 21)	234 degrees

These results provided by SkyMap Pro are in agreement with calculations for Carnac published by others (Wood, 1978, p. 140). The noteworthy event shown in Table 1 is that the positions of the rising and setting full moon are located at 90 degrees to each other during the summer solstice in 2006 and at other maximal standstill points over the 18.6-year cycle of moon positions. This is not true for the winter solstice, or for the summer solstice during other years (e.g. in 1996 the setting and rising moon are at 242 and 117 degrees, respectively). This moon–moon orientation does not occur at other latitudes. The location of the cathedral at Chartres, originally occupied by some megalithic stones, is close to, but not exactly at, the latitude of Carnac.

If the neolithic observers who constructed Carnac had similar interests as the builders of Stonehenge, it seems likely that these 90-degree moon–moon angles would have had a spiritual significance to them. It might have been one reason why this particular location was chosen despite the tremendous effort of erecting all these stones. To our knowledge, no other investigator has noticed that the latitude of Carnac is required to observe these events, in spite of all the publications showing the details of astronomical alignments of standing stones. Is it just a coincidence, or was Carnac, like Stonehenge, positioned at a specific location to commemorate an astronomical event?

Why is it that the sun and moon were considered worthy of so much effort and worship? In addition to the obvious religious attraction of objects in the sky, the focus on solely the moon and sun seem to point to a philosophy of dualism, that of contrasting a bright, constant object (sun) with that of a pale, changeable object (moon). This duality in thinking may extend to another dual contrast: male vs. female. Many observers of megalithic sites have noted that frequently, large stones are placed as pairs. Often, one stone is tall and slender, while the other may be shorter and broader, taking the form of a triangle or rounded boulder (Burl, 1993, p. 192). It is not unreasonable to propose that these pairs of stones symbolize the two sexes. Moreover, there is a direct symbolic connection between the moon and the female sex.

It has been observed that the reproductive cycle of women, with a period lasting twenty-eight days, shows a rhythm similar to the interval between full moons (29.5 days). In fact, the term "menstrual cycle" derives from the Latin for "moon." Ancient peoples regarded this as a mystical connection between the moon and the female principal. Nowadays, we tend to dismiss this as mere coincidence and superstition. But are we correct in doing so?

The reproductive cycles of mammals show a great diversity between species. In some species such as horses, donkeys, and cats, breeding and ovulation only occur during the spring, and appear to be stimulated by the longer periods of daylight that occur after the spring equinox. In other animals like goats, deer, and sheep, reproductive cycling only begins in the autumn with the onset of shorter periods of daylight (Bentley, 1982, p. 350). In animals such as rats, which breed throughout the year and which have cycles only four days long, numerous experiments have shown that exposing an animal to very dim, continuous illumination causes infertility. The effects of photoperiod upon the reproductive system partly arise because illumination sends signals from the retina to the brain and pineal gland, which respond by varying the secretion of a hormone called melatonin that can affect pituitary function. Studies in humans have also revealed an influence of photoperiod upon the menstrual cycle (Wetterberg, 1993). Possibly, if one of our primate ancestors were primarily nocturnal, the main influence of ambient light could have arisen from moonlight, which does show twenty-nine

day periods of variation. So perhaps the mystic connection between the moon and the female principal may have some foundation in reality!

Finally, the very name of Carnac cannot fail to attract our
curiosity. It mimics the name of another site replete with stone
obelisks and dedicated to the worship of the sun—the Egyptian
temple complex at Karnak. Is this yet another coincidence, or is it
possible that ancient peoples of Brittany could have heard stories
or rumors, if not direct communications, about the sacred site in
faraway Egypt and named their own sacred locale in imitation of
it? This is not quite so farfetched as it sounds. There is evidence,
for example, that Phoenician vessels originating in the Middle East
traded with locations in Spain as early as 1000 B.C. Also, sunken
vessels found in the Mediterranean and dating from about 2000
B.C. have been found to contain amber jewelry that could only
have originated in the distant Baltic Sea (Poe, 1997, p. 15). So it
is not impossible that some knowledge of sites in Egypt could
have been carried to Brittany. However, since the basis for this
name in France is no longer known, and since the name may be
more recent than the megalithic stones, there is no certain way of
understanding this riddle.

As we continue with our story, we will try to show that
Callanish, Stonehenge, and Carnac are only several examples of
other monuments that are geographically located to fit into an
ancient scheme of astronomical observation. Let us continue by
looking at other sites.

Germany

The Externsteine

As stated earlier, the rationale for the location of the most impressive megalithic site in Britain, Stonehenge, appears to have been the detection of a 90-degree angle between the summer sun and moon at this latitude. If we examine continental Europe at this latitude, are there any analogous sites?

One site of interest is the Externsteine, a natural rock formation of five enormous sandstone pillars jutting up 100 feet out of the ground north of Dortmund in Germany (Matthes, 1982; Westwood, 1996) (Fig. 6). This site is surrounded by numerous megalithic standing stones and/or associated medieval churches that in some instances were located so as to "line up" in straight lines, *Heilige Linien,* that can be traced for many kilometers across the landscape. The rock formations themselves bear many picturesque carvings created in both pre-Christian and medieval times. At the top of one of the stone pillars, which allows a wide view of the surrounding countryside (and of course, the horizon), a circular "window" has been carved right through the rock. Through this window, the sunrise at the summer solstice and also the most northerly rising of the full moon can be viewed. This suggests that the stone carvers who altered these natural rocks were interested in the same astronomical phenomena observed at Stonehenge. However, since the latitude of the Externsteine is just short of 52 degrees north the sun-moon angle at this natural site of venerated stones is not precisely 90 degrees.

Fig. 6

Map of Germany

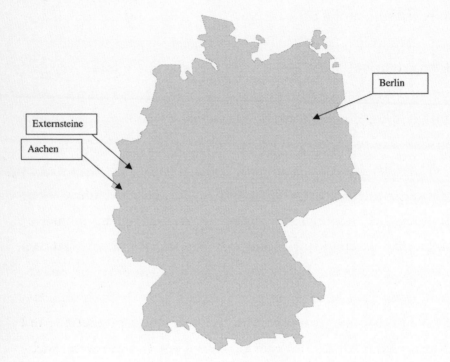

Pagan worship at the Externsteine continued into historic times; even though the great king Charlemagne, in his lifelong efforts to supplant paganism, forbid this worship at the site in A.D. 772. Much later, in A.D. 1120, Cistercian monks carved a depiction of the descent from the Cross into the rock of the Externsteine that also depicted the triumph of Christianity over symbols of the pagan religion such as the *Irminsul,* or pagan Tree of Life. The record of the involvement of Charlemagne with the

Externsteine is of interest, since there is now evidence that he might have shown a similar concern for a site located more exactly at the latitude of Stonehenge.

The Cathedral at Aachen

In northwestern Germany, there is a middle-sized city named Aachen with a population of about 180,000 and a fairly typical mixture of old and new German architecture. About 1200 years ago, however, this city was chosen by Charlemagne, King of the Franks, to be the capital of the Holy Roman Empire, the largest European state since the Roman Empire. Charlemagne's rule of his empire, which included most of France, Germany, and northern Italy, was marked by political stability, prosperity, and an encouragement of the arts and learning. The clear and esthetically pleasing Carolingian script was devised for the writing of manuscripts, and libraries and schools connected with the royal palace were established as well; collections of manuscripts in the libraries allowed the survival of many classical works written by Caesar, Cicero, and others.

Hermann Weisweiler, an amateur historian well aware of the past glories of Aachen, became further intrigued about its history after reading Hawkins's book about Stonehenge (Weisweiler, 1981). He noted that the latitude of Stonehenge was 51.1 degrees north of the equator, while that for Aachen was similar (50.84 degrees north of the equator). Aachen possesses the most famous and best-preserved remnant of Charlemagne's Holy Roman Empire—

the Aachen cathedral, constructed in A.D. 792. after the instructions of Charlemagne, whose tomb is within the cathedral itself. Many of the architectural features of the cathedral appear to be modeled after those of a cathedral in Ravenna, Italy. Weisweiler decided to examine this jewel of Charlemagne's capital city for any similarities to the site at Stonehenge. His examination does appear to bear fruit.

The main feature of the Aachen cathedral is a cylindrical portion surmounted by a large dome. This part of the cathedral seems to have been constructed with close attention to geometrical principles: Its outer walls enclose a circle with a diameter of about thirty-five meters, which is about equal to the height of this portion. This allows the whole construction to fit precisely within the confines of an imaginary cube. Within the cathedral, eight marble pillars form an octagon with a diameter of about twenty meters. When the floor plan of the Aachen cathedral is overlaid upon the plan of Stonehenge as seen from above, the two plans correspond exactly: The outer circle fits exactly upon the outline of the Sarsen stone circle, and the octagon fits exactly upon the Sarsen stone "horseshoe" pattern (Fig. 1 vs. Fig. 7). This correspondence could easily be dismissed as mere coincidence. However, other details about Aachen also show connections to astronomy and Stonehenge.

A series of windows in the cathedral just beneath the dome are positioned to allow specific astronomical sightings. The angle required to view the windows from the floor is exactly 51 degrees. This position centers the pole star at night directly in the

Fig. 7

Floor Plan of the Cathedral at Aachen

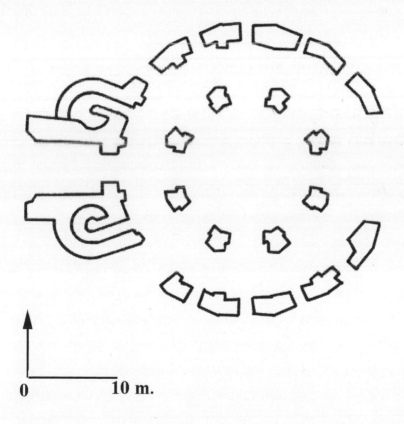

0   10 m.

north window; also, the position of the sun at noon on the days of the spring and fall equinoxes (the two times of the year when day length equals night length) also makes a 51 degree angle with the horizon and is visible through the south window of the cathedral. Finally, a view of a map of the Aachen area shows that six structures—a pre-Christian burial mound, an old fountain, the church of St. Jacob, the Aachen cathedral, the church of St. Peter, and a church in nearby Haaren—lie along a straight line pointing to the rising sun on the day of the summer solstice. This is the same line marked out at Stonehenge and occupied by a ditch-bordered "avenue." It is possible that all six of these old structures just happen to fall on this straight line purely by chance. However, what is the likelihood that such an "accidental" straight line points precisely to the rising sun during the summer solstice?

If, on the map, you draw a line at a right angle (90 degrees) to this line from the cathedral, it points to the maximal "standpoint" in the 18.6-year cycle of the rising moon on the day of the summer solstice (141 degrees away from true north) and intersects a medieval tower called the Grannusturm (Fig. 8) (Weisweiler, 1981, p. 123). Weisweiler also notes that a number of very old structures are positioned around the cathedral so that they lie on the circumferences of imaginary circles that can be drawn around it. The Grannusturm lies on one of these circles; another, outer circle around the cathedral contains the church of St. Peter and a Templar grave. All of these data show that a number of structures

Fig. 8

Alignment of Medieval Structures of Aachen

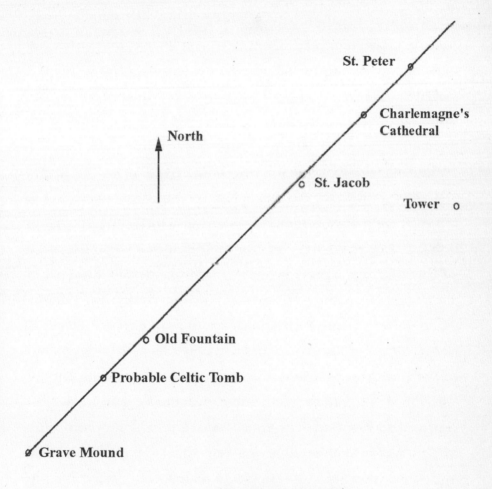

After Weisweiler, 1981

around the cathedral were deliberately positioned in accord with abstract geometrical and astronomical principles.

The data uncovered by Weisweiler—the shared latitude, the similarities in structure between Stonehenge and the cathedral, and the astronomical alignments—convinced him that the astronomical/architectural features of Stonehenge (or perhaps a megalithic construction at Aachen that had resembled Stonehenge) had been deliberately incorporated into the structure of the Aachen cathedral. But how? And why?

Just as at the Externsteine and at Chartres, it seems likely that pre-Christian features of the site had been incorporated into the cathedral and neighboring churches in an effort to replace pagan symbols with those of Christianity. This was a well-recognized policy of Charlemagne, noteworthy in his battles with the pagan Saxons, who were forcibly converted to Christianity when on the losing side of a battle. Also, knowledge of Stonehenge itself could have been transmitted to Aachen through a learned cleric, Alcuin of York, who orchestrated the intellectual accomplishments of Charlemagne's empire. Alcuin, a native Englishman, had been recruited to come to Aachen to oversee theological and other matters, and was known to have a wide range of philosophical and intellectual interests. For example, in his Epistula 170, written to Charlemagne, Alcuin discusses the timing of the various phases of the moon over the year (Alberi, 1989).

Many other sites in northern and central Europe repeat the themes seen at Stonehenge and in Germany. As far away as central

Romania, in the capital of ancient Dacia—Sarmizegetusa—a large stone circle with a central stone "horseshoe" arrangement of stones was built that has striking similarities with Stonehenge. Instead of pointing toward sunrise at the summer solstice, however, the axis of this monument points to sunrise at the winter solstice (Krupp, 1994, p. 228).

These examples show that ceremonial sites of ancient peoples throughout Europe often marked astronomical alignments with the sun and moon, and that many of these sites are still preserved in the guise of cathedrals and monuments that were later built over them. The locations of Stonehenge, ceremonial sites at the Externsteine, and the cathedral at Aachen at the same latitude of about 51 degrees north reflect the unique sun–moon angle that can be observed only at this latitude. Templar constructions can be detected in the neighborhoods of all these places—e.g., at Avebury, Carnac, and Aachen. This linkage between megalithic astronomy and later religious structures may help explain the mysterious features of other sites at more southerly latitudes.

CHAPTER 3

Mysterious Architecture of Rennes-le-Chateau

RENNES-LE-CHATEAU IS A SMALL VILLAGE PERCHED ON A mountaintop in a beautiful region of southern France, close to the town of Quillan and not far from the border with Spain (Fig. 9). Life in this village has been peaceful and seemingly unremarkable until the early 1970s, when the English journalist Henry Lincoln and his associates began producing a series of television programs and books that brought hundreds of thousands of visitors to this small village. Lincoln had uncovered evidence of mysterious, newly discovered parchments hinting at hidden treasure, dark secrets of a distant past, and a secret society connected with the Knights Templar that may still persist to this day. All these elements of a very complicated story, which I want to review individually in this book, have been greeted with a mixture of excitement and skepticism. Some of the most striking features of Lincoln's story,

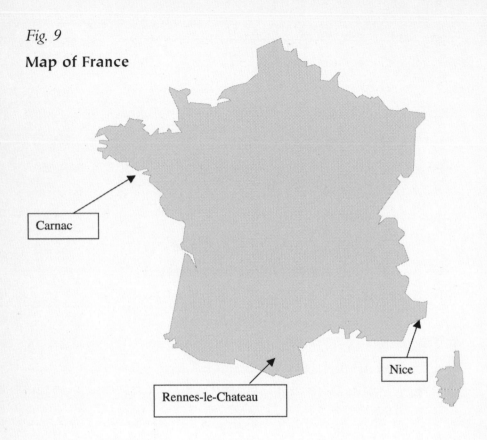

Fig. 9

Map of France

however, are undeniable and can be easily confirmed by simply looking at a map: The location of churches and castles in the area of Rennes-le-Chateau create huge, geometric patterns.

Geometry and Rennes-le-Chateau

Lincoln uncovered the geometric alignments of churches and castles in the area of Rennes-le-Chateau by inspection of highly accurate maps published by the National Geographic Institute of France (1:25,000 scale). Lincoln also confirmed some of these alignments by direct observations from points in the area itself. A small-scale version of the relevant map is published on the inside cover of the 1991 book by Lincoln; also, an excellent copy of these maps is available on a CD-ROM published by Martha Neyman (Neyman, 1998; http://wanadoo.be/rlcbooks). I have used a copy of these maps to examine the locations on my own, and have done my best to transpose the data onto Fig. 10 as accurately as I could.

Fig. 10

Churches and Castles Near Rennes-le-Chateau

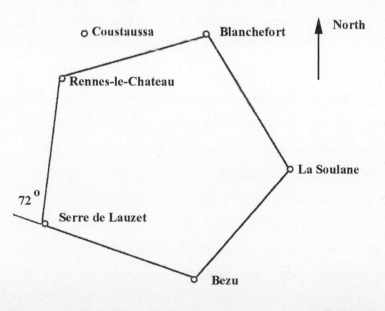

One of the first things that Lincoln noted was that lines drawn between the church in the mountaintop village of Rennes-le-Chateau, a Templar castle at a location called Bezu, and another mountaintop Templar castle called Blanchefort formed a perfect triangle with two equal sides and internal angles of 36, 72, and 72 degrees. This type of triangle can be used as the basis of a pentagon.

And sure enough, if lateral extensions from the points of this triangle are drawn, they intersect to form a pentagon with lateral points centered on a hilltop to the east called La Soulane and the end of a rising crest to the west called Serre de Lauzet. Thus, a perfectly symmetrical pentagon some fifteen miles in circumference and marked out by mountaintop structures or features is formed. As Lincoln noted, fires lit at the tops of these points could all be easily seen at night (Lincoln, 1991, p. 67) . In addition, close to the geometric center of this pentagon is another mountain called La Pique (Lincoln, 1991, p. 71).

Other writers on this subject, Richard Andrews and Paul Schellenberger, have noted that the castles at Blanchefort and Arques, together with a church at Peyrolles, form the points of a perfect 30-60-90 degree triangle; this is also confirmed by inspection of the map (Andrews, 1997, p. 243). Another point is that the church at Rennes-le-Chateau, the castle at Blanchefort, and the church at the village of Arques to the east all fall on a straight line; a village tradition in the area contends that this line points to the rising sun on the morning of July 22, St. Mary Magdalene's day

(Lincoln, 1991, p. 75). The church at Rennes-le-Chateau is dedicated to Mary Magdalene.

There is always a danger in this type of speculation that an observer is imposing an order on the points on a map that do not reflect reality. However, there are many other alignments that also indicate a large-scale geometry. Lines drawn from the points of the pentagon through the center also point to a castle in the village of Montferrand and to another church in another nearby village (Lincoln, 1991, p. 93). Ten lines through sixteen structures in the general area all converge on a point in the village of Rennes-le-Chateau. All of these alignments, in addition to others proposed by Lincoln, seem too numerous to be coincidental.

What is the meaning of these geometrical alignments of churches and castles, many of which are almost a thousand years old? How and why were these pentagonal (and star-shaped) patterns constructed? Are they related in any way to megalithic astronomy? Obviously, I wouldn't have written this book if I didn't feel that some of these puzzling aspects of this region of southern France could be related to pre-Christian astronomical alignments. But how does one examine this question?

One approach would be to examine astronomical alignments of some of these structures using the computer software described in Chapter 2 for the latitude (42.7 degrees north of the equator) of Rennes-le-Chateau.

The astronomical data applicable to Rennes-le-Chateau can be summarized in two tables, illustrating the positions of the moon at the minimal standstill point of the 18.6-year cycle and also at the maximal standstill point.

If these orientations are analyzed, what are the results? For one thing, at the minimal standstill points (as in 1997), the angle between the summer moonrise (115 degrees) and winter sunset (237 degrees) amounts to about 122 degrees. If this angle is bisected, the result is 61 degrees, close to 60 degrees, which can be used to construct an equilateral triangle or a 30-60-90 degree triangle. More interestingly, at the maximal standstill point in 2006, the angle between the rising moon (51 degrees) and rising sun (123 degrees) at the winter solstice is exactly 72 degrees, an angle complimentary to the angle formed at the points of a pentagon. During the summer solstice, the angle between moonset and sunset is, according to my calculations, about 71 degrees. Only at this latitude north of the equator can these sun-moon angles be used to construct a pentagon. At the latitude of Stonehenge, the sun-moon angle was used to construct another polygon: a rectangle.

Do these abstract angles bear any relationship to the actual structures present on the ground in the region of Rennes-le-Chateau? Some interesting correspondences are shown in Fig. 11. The line through Rennes-le-Chateau and the church at Peyrolles points to the rising full moon during the winter solstice (maximal standpoint). The line between Rennes-le-Chateau and the church at Serres points exactly to the rising full moon during the winter solstice at the minimal standpoint of the moon.

Table 2

Lunar and Solar Locations on the Horizon at the Minimal Standstill Point for Rennes-le-Chateau

Summer Solstice, 1997

Full Moonrise	115 degrees from true north
Full Moonset	244 degrees
Sunrise	58 degrees
Sunset	302 degrees

Winter Solstice, 1997

Full Moonrise	65 degrees
Full Moonset	295 degrees
Sunrise	123 degrees
Sunset	237 degrees

Table 3

Lunar and Solar Locations on the Horizon at the Maximal Standstill Point for Rennes-le-Chateau

Summer Solstice, 2006

Full Moonrise	130.6 degrees from true north
Full Moonset	231 degrees
Sunrise	58 degrees
Sunset	302 degrees

Winter Solstice, 2006

Full Moonrise	51 degrees
Full Moonset	308 degrees
Sunrise	123 degrees
Sunset	236.5 degrees

Fig. 11

Astronomical Alignments of Structures Near Rennes-le-Chateau

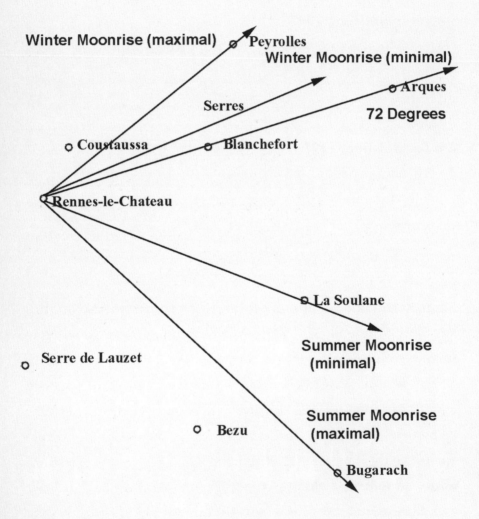

The line through Rennes-le-Chateau, Blanchefort, and Arques is oriented 72 degrees from true north. This "sunrise line" can actually be extended both to the east and west to precisely intersect additional structures. To the west, this imaginary line passes through a church at Campagne-sur-Aude, which was once the center of a so-called Commandery of the Knights Templar. To the east, the line intersects a stone cross at a location described on the map as the Templar Camp (Lincoln, 1991, p. 130). All of the sites on this line show a direct connection to the Templars.

This "sunrise line" is not the only line oriented 72 degrees from true north that can be found upon the map. Just to the south of Rennes-le-Chateau, a line drawn precisely through village churches at Laval, Le Bezu, Sougraigne, La Mouline, and Auriac is parallel to the "sunrise line" and also thus describes a 72-degree angle from true north (Lincoln, 1991, p. 129-130). Is it a mere coincidence that all of these five churches fall on a perfectly straight line pointing to this precise angle? This seems unlikely to be a chance occurrence. There is a statistical method, called a linear regression analysis, which could be applied to such a line, and would provide the "goodness of fit" of the positions of these landmarks to the straight line. Since the churches fall right upon the line, a coefficient of linearity for these five data points would undoubtedly be extremely significant statistically. But to be statistically valid, such an analysis would have to include not only these five arbitrarily chosen churches, but also the locations of all similar churches in the immediate area. Since there are at least twenty-five small churches in the area of Rennes-le-Chateau, and since only these five are near the straight line, this type of statistical analysis cannot be applied to this line and would not really be meaningful (Dixon, 1969, p. 196).

In addition to these two lines, Lincoln has identified a number of other lines through various structures and landmarks that parallel these two lines. It is hard to imagine how this complex grid of structures, geometrically tied to the pentagon of mountains, could be some sort of chance accident or a figment of an observer's imagination.

The line from Rennes-le-Chateau through the peak of La Soulane points, within 2 degrees, to full moonrise during the summer solstice at the minimal standpoint of the moon. The line running through Rennes-le-Chateau, La Pique at the center of the pentagon, and also through a church at Bugarach points at moonrise at the summer solstice at the maximal standpoint of the moon. Finally, a line from La Soulane to a church at Coustaussa points at sunset on the day of the summer solstice.

While these astronomical orientations need to be confirmed by direct observations at the actual sites at the appropriate dates in the appropriate years, these initial approximations seem to be preliminary evidence for some astronomical alignments at Rennes-le-Chateau that show an interest in a pentagonal geometry. It is always possible, of course, that these astronomical lines of sight through these selected points arise through mere coincidence. Lines drawn from Rennes-le-Chateau to many other sites would lie at different angles with no particular significance. But the line from Rennes-le-Chateau through Arques already has a tradition of astronomical significance, and the church at Peyrolles forms the point of a gigantic right triangle. These landmarks, at least, seem to have had demonstrable significance for inhabitants of the area.

The "sunrise line" proceeding from Rennes-le-Chateau through Blanchefort and the church at Arques and describing a precise 72-degree angle from true north requires a more careful examination. Lincoln reported a tradition that this sunrise line is observable on July 22, the day dedicated to Mary Magdalene. However, the computer software contradicts this tradition: At the latitude of Rennes-le-Chateau, the sun rises at a position 72 degrees from true north on about August 15, rather than July 22. August 15 is a day dedicated to another Mary: It is the day commemorating the day of the Assumption of the Virgin Mary into heaven. Is this just a coincidence? What do we know about Assumption Day, and does it bear any relationship to astronomy?

The feast of the Assumption of the Virgin Mary on August 15 is a church holiday that is not based upon scripture, but rather originates from a very old tradition within the Christian community of Jerusalem. It first appears to have been celebrated in A.D. 431, after the Council of Ephesus. By A.D. 650, it was celebrated in Rome and gradually spread throughout Europe, though apparently its observance ran into initial opposition in Gaul (France) (New Catholic Encyclopedia, 1967, p. 975).

On the date of August 15, the sun sets and rises very near to the star Regulus (Ovason, 2000, p. 346). Regulus is a very bright (magnitude 3) star and thus is quite prominent in the night sky: Out of about 1,000 stars visible to the naked eye, only about 40-50 are as bright as Regulus (King, 1967; SkyMap Pro Software, 1998). Regulus is located at one point of a right triangle formed also by two other bright stars, Spica and Arcturus. This stellar right triangle is very conspicuous in the night sky and encloses the constellation Virgo.

It may not be a coincidence that August 15, a day when the sun rises and sets near the constellation Virgo, was chosen by the Church to be dedicated to the Virgin Mary. As noted above, pre-Christian cults dedicated to a virgin did exist in ancient Europe, and very likely incorporated the constellation Virgo. It would only make sense for Christians to adopt a date connected to a pre-Christian virgin to celebrate the Virgin Mary. Early Christian communities did in fact make an explicit connection between the Virgin Mary and the constellation Virgo. Other astronomical analogies were entertained as well. For example, Christ was compared with the sun: His first miracle, that of turning water into wine, was viewed as analogous to the rising sun in springtime, which stimulates burgeoning grapes to transform spring rains into wine (Heckethorn, 1965, p. 106). There is good evidence that other dates in the Church calendar may have been chosen for similar motivations. For example, the date of Christmas, December 25, may have been adjusted to meet the astronomical conceptions of a competing religious sect, Mithraism (see Chapter 8).

Also, the "sunrise line" pointing to Regulus is itself a part of a geometrical figure: It is the hypotenuse of a right triangle formed by the locations of the church at Arques and castles at Peyrolles and at Blanchefort. Of course, any three randomly positioned structures will be located at the points of a triangle, but the odds that such a triangle will be a perfect 30-60-90 degree triangle are so low that these structures cannot have been positioned by chance alone. This right triangle on the ground mimics the appearance of the stellar right triangle formed by the stars Regulus, Arcturus, and Spica. At the latitude of Rennes-le-Chateau, this "sunrise line" pointing to the stellar triangle and to Virgo hits the horizon at a position 72 degrees away from true north. Once again, an angle of 72 degrees is required to construct a star. Rennes-le-Chateau is located precisely at the only latitude where the sun and moon at the peak year of the summer solstice form an angle of 72 degrees with each other. This latitude has an astronomical significance regarding the sun and the moon, and landmarks in this area are also aligned with a 72-degree angle from true north to point to the star Regulus and the constellation Virgo. This recurring theme of 72-degree angles, the geometry of a star or pentagon, and an orientation of markers to point to Virgo at a time of the year (August) when it is located 72 degrees from due north suggest a philosophical interest in stars and pentagons that might have had meaning to megalithic peoples.

Practitioners of a pre-Christian cult of a virgin, like the one that has been documented to exist at the site where the Chartres cathedral was later erected, could have found this astronomically significant latitude particularly symbolic of the connection between spiritual beliefs and the heavens. Construction of churches on the sites of these venerated megalithic monuments would have co-opted and redirected the spiritual feelings of the peoples living in the area to more Christian themes. It seems likely that the positions of many structures in the area of Rennes-le-Chateau reflect an interest in astronomical observations that was incorporated into later Christian constructions.

Later on in this book, we will encounter a similar triangle in another geographical location (Washington, D.C.!) that also mimics a triangle in the sky (see Chapter 9).

It seems possible that, as at Stonehenge, observers belonging to a pre-Christian society could have examined sun-moon angles at many locations and found that the pentagonal 72-degree angle between the sun and moon exists only at the general latitude of Rennes-le-Chateau. A unique, perfect natural pentagon formed by mountain peaks at precisely the correct latitude needed to observe this special sun-moon angle could have been an object of veneration by ancient peoples, particularly if some of the mountainous features of this pentagon could be used as natural markers pointing to critical positions of the moon and sun. Henry Lincoln himself has hypothesized that the geometric alignments he noted must be of great antiquity, and that the churches and castles marking them out were positioned at points that had already been marked by pre-Christian structures (Lincoln, 1991). Is there, then, any direct evidence for megalithic structures at Rennes-le-Chateau that may clarify these questions further?

CHAPTER 4

Historical Mysteries of Rennes-le-Chateau

THE ASTRONOMICAL SIGNIFICANCE OF MOST OF THE SITES we have discussed so far—e.g. Stonehenge, Carnac, and Aachen—seems clear to us now, but actually has been made apparent only by relatively recent study. At the Chartres cathedral, to be sure, there is a teasing hint of astronomy displayed in the clear window pane aligned with the summer solstice, and also in a stained glass window depicting the twelve signs of the Zodiac, a feature rather unusual for a church (Ovason, 2000, footnote 49, p. 419). For the most part, however, the astronomical significance of most European sites was forgotten and had to be rediscovered in the twentieth century. If an astronomically aligned stone circle or monument had ever been present at Aachen, its significance was suppressed, appropriated, or assimilated into a more conventional Christian orientation. The presence of a Templar gravesite several miles to the west of the Aachen cathedral suggests that Knights Templar at one time might have understood the meaning of the site, just as their constructions at Carnac and Rennes-le-Chateau indicate an interest in astronomy there (Weissweiler, 1981, p. 122).

What makes Rennes-le-Chateau unique is the possibility that the spiritual significance of the site was never truly forgotten, but was maintained as a secret for hundreds of years. Henry Lincoln's books have proposed that a historical mystery is encoded in a number of landmarks at Rennes-le-Chateau.

The Priest at Rennes-le-Chateau

Henry Lincoln first became acquainted with the village of Rennes-le-Chateau in a book by a French author, Gerard de Sede. According to de Sede, secret, encoded manuscripts were discovered by the priest of the church of Rennes-le-Chateau, Berenger Sauniere, in 1887 (Andrews, 1996, p. 13). Sauniere is at the center of a number of mysteries about the area. For example, Sauniere suddenly acquired substantial amounts of money in the late 1890s. This money allowed him to build a large country house, create a water distribution system for the village, build a tower that he called the Tour Magdala, throw lavish banquets for invited guests, and redecorate the interior of his church with colorful and even grotesque statues and puzzling symbols (Baigent, 1996, p. 25-28). Where did his unexplained wealth come from?

De Sede alleged that Sauniere's sudden wealth was connected with an accidental discovery of parchments hidden somewhere within his church. Supposedly, the parchments were hidden within a hollow interior of one of two Visigothic columns that supported the altar (Baigent, 1996, p. 33). As we shall see in later chapters, this scenario has an unmistakable connection to the traditions and ceremonies of Freemasonry, which maintains that the secrets of the Order can be sequestered within a hollow column. Clearly, this narrative of Saunière's supposed discovery of the parchments is deliberately arranged to contain this symbolic connection with Freemasonry.

The parchments allegedly consisted of four documents: a genealogy of nobles dating from A.D. 1244, a later genealogy dating from A.D. 1644, and two documents written in Latin.

The two documents in Latin have attracted the most attention. They contain excerpts from the New Testament. However, in both texts, superfluous letters have been added to the text, and lines of text have been arranged in peculiar patterns. In the shorter document (manuscript 1), some of the letters in the words have been conspicuously raised above the others. If excerpted from the text, these specific letters spell out a puzzling message in French:

"A Dagobert II roi et a sion est ce tresor et il ist la mort."

Or, in English:

"To Dagobert II king and to Sion belongs this treasure and he is there dead."

What does this peculiar passage mean? Why would anyone have concealed this message in a parchment in 1780 (De Sede claimed that this had been written by a predecessor of Sauniere's, abbot Antoine Bigou)? Who is Dagobert II and what is Sion? Could some treasure have been the source of Sauniere's wealth?

The other Latin parchment (manuscript 2) is longer and contains a message concealed by two extraordinarily complex successive methods of encipherment. The first method reorders the letters in a message by using a transposition cipher that first positions the letters of the original message on the squares of a chessboard (Andrews, 1996, p. 46; Lincoln, 1991, p. 240). A chess piece, the knight, then is moved around the board in a precise way that allows it to visit each square once and only once. Each stop of the knight on the board assigns a new position to the letter on each square. The method of achieving this mathematical puzzle was first published in the 1700s by a French analyst named de Moivre. The second portion of the encipherment uses a substitution cipher based on a keyword that had been present on a peculiar gravestone in a church at Rennes-le-Chateau. The result of this laborious encryption provides a second message in French:

"Bergere pas de tentation que Poussin Teniers gardent la clef pax DCLXXXI par la croix et ce cheval de Dieu j'acheve ce daemon de gardien a midi pommes bleues."

Or, in English:

"Shepherdess no temptation that Poussin Teniers hold the key peace 681 by the cross and this horse of God I complete this demon of the guardian at midday blue apples."

What, if any, meaning can be gleaned from these puzzling messages?

The first message refers to Dagobert II. Dagobert II was an actual historical personage, one of the last in the line of the so-called Merovingian kings who ruled portions of France between 448 and A.D. 754. The throne of these Merovingian rulers was usurped by Pepin III in 754; Pepin III's son became known as Charlemagne, the first ruler of the Holy Roman Empire. So the Merovingian kings were predecessors to a dynasty that exerted power throughout much of medieval Europe. One of Dagobert's official residences apparently was Rennes-le-Chateau (Baigent, 1996, p. 257-268). So the mention of Dagobert II in manuscript 1 seems, at least, intelligible and connected to Rennes-le-Chateau. But what should we make of the references to a treasure and to Sion?

There are other puzzling aspects of manuscript 1. Near one corner of the manuscript, there is a small triangular device; also, scattered throughout the text are puzzling little crosses. If lines are drawn through the crosses, they intersect at the tip of the triangular device to form a large triangle passing through the text. In turn, this triangle can be used to construct a pentagon (Lincoln, 1991, p. 30). Instructions for drawing a pentagon seem to have been deliberately hidden within this message. Pentagons—connecting mountaintop churches and castles, or hidden within paintings by French artists—seem to be a recurring theme in the story of Rennes-le-Chateau.

If we momentarily disregard manuscript 1 and focus our attention on manuscript 2, some additional progress can be made. One investigator, Martha Neijman, has claimed that the "horse of God" may be a reference to a huge hilltop rock formation that, when viewed from the proper angle, shows a remarkable resemblance to a horse's head (Neijman, 1998). This natural aggregation of boulders lies to the south of Rennes-le-Chateau, not far from a point of the "pentagon" (Serre de Lauzet). Another remarkable feature of it, perhaps relevant to our focus upon astronomical orientations and megalithic monuments, is that sunlight penetrates through a cleft between these rocks only on December 24, a few days after the winter solstice, on the Feast of Saint John the Evangelist, a day held in particular esteem by Masons (see Chapter 6).

Other investigators have suggested that the cross and blue apples in the message refer to an old stone cross near Rennes-le-Chateau and to a local slang for grapes in a nearby vineyard—blue apples (Andrews, 1996). Thus, manuscript 2 may refer to landmarks in the area of Rennes-le-Chateau.

"Poussin" and "Teniers" in the message would seem to refer to two French painters of the seventeenth century, David Teniers and Nicholas Poussin. It was this reference to Poussin in this encoded document that supposedly led de Sede (and later, Henry Lincoln) to examine seventeenth-century French paintings.

Paintings by Nicholas Poussin

Nicholas Poussin was a French painter who rose to prominence in the 1630s and who completed works commissioned by some of the most noteworthy patrons of the arts, including Cardinal Richelieu. His paintings depicted a variety of topics, from a version of the Last Supper to portrayals of classical figures such as Hercules and Diogenes, Orpheus and Eurydice, and Echo and Narcissus (Gowing, 1987). Interest in a possible connection between Rennes-le-Chateau and one of his paintings was first raised by the claim by Gerard de Sede that one painting, entitled *Les Bergers d'Arcadie* or *The Shepherds of Arcadia*, depicts features found in the area of Rennes-le-Chateau.

This painting, painted in about 1647, portrays Greek shepherds, dressed in classic, archaic clothing, carrying staffs and gathered around an oblong, aboveground stone tomb. An inscription on the tomb bears the words "Et in arcadia ego." The tomb portrayed in this painting, plus the contours of the mountainous horizon behind it, seem to match the appearance of an actual tomb once located to the east of Rennes-le-Chateau, between the villages of Arques and Peyrolles, at a location called les Pontils (Andrews, 1996, p. 116).

The apparent correspondence of the tomb at les Pontils to the very similar appearing tomb painted by Poussin has inspired endless speculation as to its meaning. Could an eminent French painter have really journeyed to this obscure village just to paint a scene incorporating this tomb? The les Pontils tomb was opened in the 1920s and found to be empty. Since then, the current owner of the land has destroyed the tomb to discourage the hordes of tourists and treasure-hunters that invaded the area after the publication of Lincoln's books (Lincoln, 1997, p. 62). If there is no specific content of the tomb that is of interest, did the tomb have some symbolic value? How does it relate to the "arcadia" mentioned in the painting by Poussin? Does the actual site of the tomb have any significance?

It is of interest to us that there is a megalithic standing stone positioned just across the road from the tomb (Lincoln, 1997, p. 61). Both the site of the tomb and the standing stone are located on the imaginary line connecting Rennes-le-Chateau and the castle at Serres that points exactly to full moonrise at the winter solstice at the minimal standstill point of the moon (see fig. 11, p. 62). The stone is not the only megalithic structure present in the area. Another standing stone is at the crest of a hill just above a church at St. Salvayre, six miles to the north of Rennes-le-Chateau (Lincoln, 1997, p. 216). St. Salvayre and the les Pontils tomb are located at the points of a second, irregular pentagon marked out on the map by Lincoln (Lincoln, 1991, p. 111). Also, a well-known megalithic stone called "Pierre Dressee" is located not far to the east of the tomb and is marked on the survey map of the area (Andrews, 1996, p. 156). Exactly five miles north of the church at Coustaussa, just northwest of St. Salvayre, is a megalithic tomb called "Pierre Droite Menhir" (Lincoln, 1991, p. 149). Finally, just north of Coustaussa, hundreds of beehive-shaped structures, formed of heaps of unmortared flat stones, can be found (Lincoln, 1991, p. 152).

Archaeologists have not examined the age and origin of these structures, so their significance is uncertain. All of these observations, however, show that medieval structures are built upon the sites of older, megalithic structures that perhaps were placed as some sort of markers. The tomb site at les Pontils may thus be adjacent to one of many markers in the area that have been placed within an older, pre-Christian design with evidence of astronomical alignments.

Did Poussin paint this obscure scene? Is it possible that his painting contains some sort of secret meaning? There is some valid historical evidence, discussed by Henry Lincoln and co-authors, that Poussin was in possession of a secret of some importance. In 1656, Poussin apparently disclosed a secret to a visitor, Abbe Louis Fouquet. The Abbe alluded to this secret in a letter to his brother, the minister of finance under Louis XIV (Baigent, 1996, p. 38):

> *He and I discussed certain things...which will give you...*
> *advantages which even kings would have great pains to draw*
> *from him...and furthermore, these things are so difficult to dis-*
> *cover that nothing more on this earth can prove of better fortune*
> *nor be their equal.*

Some years after receiving this letter, in September of 1661, Minister Fouquet was arrested and imprisoned for the rest of his life, charged with corruption. Curiously, his fate was connected with another mysterious prisoner. The man imprisoned along with Fouquet was the Man in the Iron Mask.

The Man in the Iron Mask was not a historical invention, but a real prisoner whose fate was first popularized by Voltaire (Noone, 1988, p. 2). Later, the character of the Man in the Iron Mask was incorporated into the novel by Alexander Dumas, which has remained popular to this day. According to the most recent work on this subject, the identity of the Man in the Iron Mask was one Eustache d'Angers, who was first imprisoned on the island of St. Marguerite, south of Nice, in 1669, apparently because he knew of some secret that was a threat to the reign of Louis XIV (Noone, p. 252). This prisoner was actually forced to wear a mask of some sort, primarily when he was being transferred between prisons or quarters. Although the prisoner was forbidden to divulge his secret, he was nevertheless allowed to serve Fouquet during his imprisonment in the capacity of a valet. Apparently, Minister Fouquet was imprisoned for a variety of reasons, not the least being that his accumulated wealth and grandiose chateaux eclipsed the style of Louis XIV himself and infuriated him. But the possibility that some secret could also have been a reason for Fouquet's fate cannot be dismissed.

Louis XIV apparently also went to considerable effort to obtain the original Poussin painting of the tomb and kept it in his private apartments (Gowing, 1987, p. 363). So it seems likely that Poussin and his painting must have had some considerable, hidden significance. In view of the fate of Fouquet, prudence must have dictated that disclosure of the secret could only be made to a few people and with great care!

Henry Lincoln maintains that a pentagonal geometry is concealed within the dimensions and lines of Poussin's Rennes-le-Chateau painting. This seems to be confirmed by analyzing the overall dimensions of the painting: If a diagonal line between the opposite corners of the painting is drawn, it forms an angle of 36 degrees; doubling this angle and drawing intersecting lines creates a symmetrical star (Lincoln, 1991, p. 64). One curious feature of the painting was detected by X-rays that revealed that the staffs held by the shepherds in the painting apparently were painted *before* the shepherds and other features of the painting were completed (Lincoln, 1991, p. 61)! This suggests that the positioning of the staffs on the canvas was more crucial to the artist than any of the other details. One of the shepherds' staffs is positioned at a 72-degree angle from vertical and is parallel to a side of the pentagon forming the center of the imaginary star that can be superimposed on the painting (Andrews, 1996, p. 111). Also, if a line is drawn through one of the other shepherds staffs, it precisely intersects the top point of the imaginary star. Poussin did indeed appear to conceal a pentagonal geometry within his painting that is confirmed by hidden clues in the positioning of the shepherds' staffs.

Are there any additional clues in the known life and work of Poussin that would indicate an interest in or knowledge of a spiritual secret?

One work by Poussin, painted in about 1637, is of potential interest. It is entitled *The Assumption of the Virgin*. It was first acquired by Vincenzo Giustiniani and subsequently was purchased by Henry Cecil, the first marquess of Exeter. It remained in the possession of the Cecil family for over two hundred years until it was sold to the National Gallery of Art in Washington, D.C., in 1962.

The painting shows the Virgin Mary, assisted by cherubs, ascending into heaven from a rectangular, aboveground stone tomb (New Catholic Encyclopedia, vol. 1, p. 975; see plate 8). This stone tomb does not precisely match the appearance of the tomb in the other Poussin painting, *The Shepherds of Arcadia*. For example, the top corners of the tomb are not beveled, but form ordinary 90-degree angles. However, the overall proportions of this Assumption tomb (length to height = 2.3 to 1) match the proportions of the Shepherds' tomb. Also, a careful count of the cherubs in the painting, some of which are almost obscured by clouds, reveals that Poussin painted exactly fifteen cherubs supporting Mary on her journey into heaven, undoubtedly a not-so-subtle reference to the date of Assumption Day, August 15. The lighting scheme of the painting suggests that sunrise is occurring in the background of the tomb. As we have noted in the previous chapter, the rising sun on August 15 points to a stellar triangle enclosing the constellation of Virgo.

The figures in the painting show a high degree of order in their placement, as is true of many Poussin paintings: For example, the eye of Mary is located at the precise vertical midpoint of the painting. Also, due to the overall dimensions of the painting, corner-to-corner diagonal lines strike 36-degree angles relative to the long axis of the painting.

As for the *The Shepherds of Arcadia* painting, this diagonal line also allows a pentagon to be constructed. Poussin seems to have wanted to direct the attention of an observer to these diagonal

Fig. 12

Pentagonal Geometry in Poussin's *Assumption of the Virgin*.

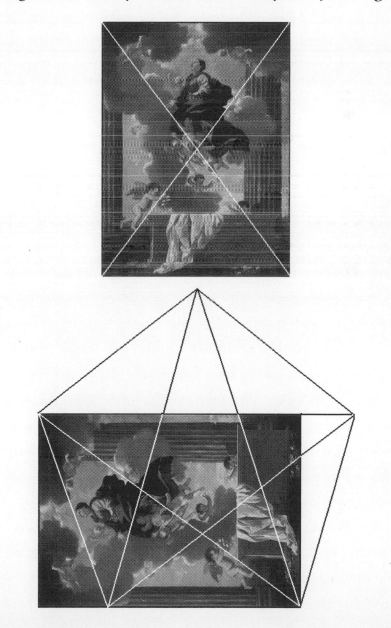

lines: One diagonal cuts through the hands and feet of a cherub, and the overall axis of this cherub is perfectly parallel to this 36-degree angle diagonal line. The other corner-to-corner diagonal cuts through the hands and feet of two other cherubs. Also, when a pentagon and interior star are projected onto the painting, one of the lines of the pentagon passes along a line connecting the head of a cherub with Mary's forehead. A cherub seems to be pointing directly at this line. Another line of the star forms a precise diagonal from one corner of the tomb to the other.

These suggestions of a pentagonal geometry, while not quite as convincing as the clear positioning of the shepherds' staffs in the *The Shepherds of Arcadia* painting, do seem to indicate a rigorous, but hidden, geometrical design. Why would Poussin have incorporated a geometry of a hidden star into his paintings? Possibly, Poussin might simply have found the overall proportions to be generally pleasing and not specifically related to some coded geometrical message. Or, perhaps the star symbolized some philosophy that was important to him. A star figures prominently in Masonic symbolism—is it possible that Poussin was acquainted with some sort of early form of Freemasonry?

Poussin's paintings would nonetheless seem to confirm that Poussin deliberately incorporated great geometrical precision and hidden symbolic messages in his works. Even the inclusion of two Ionic marble columns in *The Assumption of the Virgin* could refer to Masonic symbolism (the two Masonic columns symbolizing the two pillars on the porch of the Temple of Jerusalem) that was already well known in the early 1600s (see Chapters 5 and 6).

Could this Assumption painting be another example of a hidden interest in star symbolism and geometry by Poussin? Or is the subject of the painting unrelated and merely coincidental? Most artists have not included a tomb in their depictions of the Assumption of Mary, although a fourteenth-century work by Paolo de Giovanni Fei and a fifteenth century work by Botticelli do include tombs. It would be unusual to portray a tomb because Catholic dogma does not state clearly that the Virgin Mary actually died before her Assumption into heaven (Apostolos-Cappadona, 1994, p. 42). The subject matter of the painting is also unusual for Poussin. The forty-eight paintings he completed between 1625 and 1650 mainly portray landscapes, scenes of classical mythology, some historical Roman scenes, and a few portrayals of events in the Old Testament. Only seven of his paintings relate to New Testament themes, and only two portray the Virgin Mary.

The Shepherds of Arcadia was not the only painting by Poussin depicting shepherds, symbols of death, and arcadia. A previous painting, *Et in Arcadia Ego,* showed similar elements, though it did not depict a tomb like that at les Pontils. This painting, painted in 1630, is currently owned by the Duke of Devonshire. Also, a copy of *The Shepherds of Arcadia* painting, sculpted as a bas-relief in stone, was created in the eighteenth century and can now be found in Shugborough Hall in Staffordshire County, England

(Lincoln, 1997, p. 78). Shugborough Hall was owned by Lord Anson and is located close to Chatsworth, home of the Duke of Devonshire, who owned the original *The Shepherds of Arcadia* in the 1750s. It is likely that the bas-relief at Shugborough Hall was copied from the original when it was located nearby. When George Anson died in 1762, a poem was read aloud in Parliament that directly referred to this bas-relief, suggesting that the Anson family held the theme of *The Shepherds of Arcadia* in particular esteem (Baigent, 1996, p. 191).

Shugborough Hall was also, at one time, a home to another painting by David Teniers, the other painter referred to in the Sauniere parchments (Andrews, 1996, p. 203). Is this a coincidence, or has there been some long-standing connection between the Poussin and Teniers paintings? The Teniers painting, *Saint Anthony and Saint Jerome in the Desert,* shows no obvious similarities in appearance or theme to the Poussin painting. Teniers does seem to have a tenuous personal connection to the Templars and the Crusades: His wife, Isabelle de Fren, was closely associated with a family descended from Godfrey de Bouillon, the first Crusader ruler of Jerusalem (Andrews, 1996, p. 353).

Finally, Poussin was not the only painter to incorporate the words "Et in Arcadia Ego" into his works: The Italian painter Il Guercino created a painting with the same title in 1618 (Andrews, p. 105). This would suggest that at least a restricted circle of cognoscenti of the seventeenth century found some meaning in this phrase. But what does it mean?

"Et in Arcadia Ego" is a Latin phrase meaning "And in Arcadia I." Aside from being brief, this phrase is incomplete, lacking a verb. Lincoln has suggested that it is an anagram: If the letters are re-arranged, it can be made to say, in Latin, "I tego arcana Dei," or "I conceal the secrets of God" (Baigent, 1996, p. 40). Other investigators have proposed an even more radical, secret meaning (Andrews, 1996, p. 295). One way of reading the phrase is "Arcam Dei Tengo," or "I touch the tomb of God." Even more speculatively, these authors suggest that the Latin phrase is incomplete, and that a verb should be added to it. The most logical verb is "sum" ("am" in English, to make the phrase "And in Arcadia I am"). If the phrase is completed by adding "sum" to it, it becomes upon rearrangement, "Arcam Dei Iesus Tengo" or "I touch the tomb of God, Jesus."

This latter message is intriguing, if only because it accurately reflects what one shepherd in the Poussin painting is actually doing, i.e., touching a tomb. Of course, the message is deeply offensive to Christians who believe in the Ascension of Christ directly into heaven. Is it likely that Poussin would have composed a painting with a secret message that is so opposed to the Church and values of orthodox Christianity? About the only thing these anagrams prove is that the letters of a puzzling message can be rearranged to form even more bizarre messages. The real meaning of the message, if any hidden meaning of the phrase "Et in Arcadia ego" does indeed exist, remains obscure.

Curiously, the phrase "Et in Arcadia ego" did not disappear after the creation of these paintings. As Lincoln notes, it is repeated on an eighteenth-century gravestone near Rennes-le-Chateau investigated by the Abbe Sauniere. Also, a chapter in the well-known work by the prominent English writer, Evelyn Waugh, *Brideshead Revisited,* bears this unexplained title (Waugh, 1982). This novel, first published just after World War II, concerns the preoccupations of an elite, wealthy English family with the religious requirements of Catholic orthodoxy. Waugh had a colorful life, converting to Catholicism in 1930 following a divorce, and he traveled extensively in Africa and South America. During his wartime enlistment in the Army, he was an associate of Randolph Churchill, Winston Churchill's son, on a high-level military assignment in Yugoslavia in which he served as a liaison officer between the British Army and resistance groups. It is unknown why this orthodox, serious Catholic writer would have employed this precise phrase in his novel (Hastings, 1994, p. 484).

These and other traces of this enigmatic phrase in other works of art suggest that some esoteric meaning of "Et in Arcadia ego" has been recognized and preserved through the years by a select number of individuals. This meaning still has not been made clear to the rest of us. At the very least, the attention paid to Poussin and his artwork, as a result of Henry Lincoln's books, has uncovered some very interesting and unexplained aspects of art and literary history. Poussin clearly was in possession of some secret knowledge, incorporated hidden geometric themes into his paintings, and appears to have pursued an unorthodox philosophy that was hinted at in his artwork.

Do the works of Poussin, however, directly point to a mystery at Rennes-le-Chateau? This question is partly dependent upon the identity and history of the tomb at Rennes-le-Chateau allegedly painted by Poussin. Baigent and Lincoln expressed the opinion that the tomb was indeed very old, and stated that it was acquired in 1930 by an American named Louis Lawrence, of Boston, Massachusetts, who apparently died during the 1950s (Baigent, 1996, p. 40).

I have tried to examine this claim by consulting a number of online databases operated by the U.S. Census bureau, public record sites of various states of New England, and by the Church of the Latter Day Saints, which is particularly interested in tracing ancestry and genealogy. Many Louis Lawrences are listed in these databases, but none with a death date in the 1950s hailed from Boston or some other New England state. One Boston family appeared to be of interest: that descending from Samuel Crocker Lawrence, born in Medford, Massachusetts, in 1832. Mr. Lawrence graduated from Harvard, served in the Civil War in the Battle of Bull Run, and as a prosperous businessman later in life, served as a Grand Commander of the Knights Templar Masonic organization of Massachusetts. He had an extensive library of Masonic lore, which he donated to the Grand Lodge of Massachusetts. As we noted above, there are traces of Masonic symbolism (documents hidden in columns) in the story of Abbe Sauniere. A book published in France in 1979 claims that Sauniere was a member of some type of Masonic organization

(Baigent, 1996, p. 205). A descendent of this Mr. Lawrence would be an interesting candidate for the owner of the tomb near Rennes-le-Chateau; however, Mr. Lawrence's own children were named Louise and William, and there is no record of either of them having lived in France (Cyclopedia of American Biography, 1967, p. 436).

Lately, a number of investigators have cast serious doubt on Baigent and Lincoln's account of the tomb and have listed their objections on the many websites that are devoted to Rennes-le-Chateau. One author, Paul Smith, has summarized his doubts in an impressive site at http://smithppO.tripod.com/psp/.d33. Smith scrutinized historical records from the area to review the evidence presented in Baigent's and de Sede's books. He found that a scholar named Louis Fedie wrote an article about the region in 1878 that described the megalithic stone at les Pontils but failed to mention any tomb at the spot. Moreover, property records state that the les Pontils site was purchased in 1880 by Louis Galibert for the preparation of a grave for his mother. In 1921, Galibert's mother was disinterred for transfer to another grave and the property and gravesite were sold to an American named Louis B. Lawrence, from Hartford, Connecticut. It was Mr. Lawrence who evidently commissioned a redesign of the tomb in 1933. So the later appearance of the tomb, which does strikingly resemble the tomb portrayed by Poussin, was completed in modern times. If this new information is true, Poussin could not in fact have painted the tomb in 1640.

These conflicting narratives, neither of which can be confirmed by U.S. public records, cast doubt upon the antiquity of
the tomb at les Pontils. It is possible that the tomb is modern and
somehow was deliberately designed to resemble the tomb in *The
Shepherds of Arcadia* by Poussin. But the motivation for such an act
is unclear. Alternatively, the similarity between the les Pontils
tomb and the tomb in *The Shepherds of Arcadia* might have only
been coincidental and perhaps was misleadingly utilized by the
authors of the numerous books on Rennes-le-Chateau to connect the mysterious painting by Poussin to an unremarkable
burial site in the village.

In addition, a number of investigators have charged that the
mysterious parchments allegedly found by Sauniere were in fact
manufactured by Phillipe de Cherisey in the 1950s. If so, de
Cherisey must have had a remarkable facility for languages and an
exceptional skill at cryptography to create such a complicated
manuscript. Such an effort, moreover, yielded messages with
obscure references to Dagobert II and "blue apples," wording that
is scarcely intelligible. If the parchments are in fact forgeries,
someone went to a great deal of trouble to produce a meager and
mystifying result.

If these criticisms prove valid, the apparent historical connection between the les Pontils tomb and the Poussin tomb was an
invention of de Sede and his associate, Pierre Plantard. Plantard
was known to have participated in a right wing, Masonic-like
movement during the 1940s called Alpha Galates (Latin for "First

Gauls") that embraced esoteric and Masonic symbolism (Baigent, 1986, p. 323).

What remains puzzling about Rennes-le-Chateau, regardless of the veracity of the story of Sauniere's parchments or the connection to Poussin, is why ancient churches in the area appear to be arranged in large geometric patterns, and why the Templar castles of Blanchefort and Bezu occupy critical positions in these patterns.

Another intriguing facet of the Rennes-le-Chateau story is the proposal by Lincoln and co-workers that it is a site of origin of a secret society, the Priory of Sion, that has awarded membership to numerous highly influential people and has striven to achieve hidden political goals for centuries. This society claims to have originated in the Knights Templar and is allied in some way with Freemasonry. How plausible are these claims?

To examine these claims further, we must examine the history of two communities of people with unique, shared values that were brutally suppressed during the thirteenth and fourteenth centuries: the Cathars and the Knights Templar.

CHAPTER 5

Lost Societies of Medieval France

The Cathars

As discussed by Lincoln and by another author on the subject, Jeff Merrifield (Merrifield, 1995), the Cathars of southern France were a local, unorganized community with unorthodox but Christian religious beliefs. One of the few surviving documents to describe Cathar principles was written in A.D. 1230 by an Italian, John of Lugio, and was entitled the "Book of Two Principles." According to this book, the Cathars advocated vegetarianism, sexual continence, and reverence for Jesus. However, they did not recognize the necessity for priests to interpret scripture, and did not revere the image of the Cross, disparaging it as the instrument of torture for Jesus.

The Cathars inhabited the culturally distinct region of Langue-doc, which surrounds the area occupied by Rennes-le-Chateau and neighboring towns and villages. This region derives its name from the distinct French dialect spoken in this region, in which the word for "yes" was "oc" rather than "oui." Accordingly, this region was called the "Land of Oc" or Languedoc in French. The cultural and religious idiosyncrasies of the Cathars inhabiting this area apparently were tolerated for hundreds of years after the introduction of Christianity in France. The early origin of Cathar thought is uncertain, though it has been demonstrated that there were communications between the Cathars and a somewhat similar, unorthodox religious community arising in Bulgaria and present-day Bosnia called the Bogomils.

The early era of toleration of unorthodox Cathar beliefs came to an end in A.D. 1208. In this year, Pope Innocent III wrote a Bull of Anathema against the Cathars, calling for a Crusade to eliminate this heresy. By July, 1209, a large army of mainly northern French soldiers had assembled near Beziers and reportedly massacred 20,000 people in the region. While some resistance persisted for a few decades, a final revolt at the castle of Montsegur in 1242 was forcefully suppressed and the Cathar heresy was officially eliminated. Rennes-le-Chateau itself played no special role in this event, but is located within thirty miles of Montsegur and must have been included in the Cathar tragedy (Lincoln, 1997, p. 106). The whole episode is also referred to as the Albigensian Crusade, since much of the activity was centered around a town in the Languedoc called Albi. Those inhabitants of the area who were not put to the sword were forced to either conceal or abandon their religious ideas.

Curiously, this general area of France has also become associated with another unique religious phenomenon. About 100 miles west of Rennes-le-Chateau is the village of Lourdes. Like many villages in this area, Lourdes is dominated by a castle, Mirambel, which is located on a mountaintop overlooking the village. In A.D. 778, Charlemagne attacked this castle and seized it from its Muslim occupiers, restoring this area of France to Christendom. This historical footnote, however, is not the reason for the renown of Lourdes.

Lourdes derives its fame from events reported beginning in February of 1858. In this year, a 14-year-old girl, Bernadette Soubirous, experienced numerous visions of the Virgin Mary at a grotto (the entrance to a cave) near the banks of the river Gave. Her visions were at first greeted with considerable skepticism by the local priests, Abbe Pomian and Abbe Serres. However, the townspeople reverently accepted her testimony, and soon thousands of people accompanied her to witness her visions at the grotto, which were perceptible to her alone (Trochu, 1985). Since then, Lourdes has attracted thousands of pilgrims who believe in the sanctity and healing properties of the site. What is noteworthy about Lourdes is that it represents an example of direct contact between man and God, without an intervening mediation of the Church. The ready acceptance of such a phenomenon by the local population is reminiscent of the much earlier Cathar disregard for the formal institutions of religion.

The Crusades and the Founding of the Knights Templar

An organization that may have given shelter to both the ideas of Catharism and to persecuted Cathars themselves was the Knights Templar. This fabled organization, which continues to fascinate many students of history today, is inextricably associated with the mass movements of faith and military might that became known as the Crusades. In order to understand the Templars, it is necessary to understand the Crusades (Howarth, 1982; Payne, 2000).

The main object of the Crusades was to recover the Holy City of Jerusalem from the infidel Muslims. Jerusalem had naturally been an object of religious devotion since the beginning of Christianity, but in the early years, little importance was attached to actually visiting Jerusalem or viewing holy relics.

The quest for actual, physical traces of Jesus and his disciples gained momentum in A.D. 325, when Bishop Macarius of Jerusalem claimed to have discovered the site of the tomb of Jesus. One year later, the Byzantine Empress Helena traveled to the spot from Constantinople to search for the crosses of the Crucifixion, and returned home with fragments of what was believed to be the True Cross (Payne, 2000, p. 19).

For years, scholars have viewed this narrative with extreme skepticism, noting that many faked relics were distributed in Europe throughout history, and that any such relic could not possibly be genuine. More recently, however, the renowned Bible scholar Carsten Thiede has reexamined a fragment of wood called the Santa Croce Titulus ("Title Board of the Holy Cross" in Latin) that was rediscovered in the 1400s in a Roman church founded by Helena. This ancient wooden fragment bears the words "Jesus, King of the Jews" in archaic Latin and Hebrew. By analyzing the precise forms and wording on the Titulus, Thiede makes a convincing case that this wooden fragment was one of the relics recovered from Jerusalem by Helena and might just possibly be a true remnant of the Cross (Thiede, 2002).

Jerusalem, however, was lost to Christendom when it was surrendered to Muslim armies in A.D. 638 (Howarth, 1982, p. 21). Although sporadic attempts were made to recover the city, as when Byzantine armies marched upon Jerusalem in A.D. 964, none were successful. This wound to the pride of Christianity was to persist until the election of a remarkable man, Urban II, as Pope in A.D. 1088.

The French bishop who was to become Urban II was born in Chatillon-sur-Marne, France, in 1042. He spent much of his early career in the famous monastery at Cluny. Not long after being elected Pope, Urban began an intense campaign to promote the recovery of Jerusalem by force. He met with envoys from the Byzantine Emperor Alexius Comnenus, who communicated to him the plight of Christians in the Muslim Middle East. Urban II also organized a major Church council in Clermont in 1095, at which he accused Muslims of oppressing and torturing Christians. At the end of the council, he appealed to his audience for a Crusade to liberate Jerusalem, and was met with more enthusiasm than even he had been prepared to expect. Volunteers immediately began sewing cloth crosses to their clothing and started to organize armies.

The exact motives behind Urban II's proclamations are hard to assess today. Clearly, the obvious religious motivations apply. Many historians have also suggested that an unstated goal of Urban was to divert the violent energy of Europe's knights away from constant conflict with each other toward the more productive goal of recovering Jerusalem. But little evidence of his intention remains.

The wild enthusiasm generated by Urban's appeal had a number of unfortunate effects. One of these was the creation of an unorganized rabble that looked to a charismatic holy man, Peter the Hermit, as its leader. This poorly armed and undisciplined mass of men became known as the People's Crusade and by May of 1096 started off on a long march across Europe to reach the Holy Land. As they crossed Hungary and what was formerly called Yugoslavia, battles with local forces reduced Peter's men by one fourth. Finally, when they arrived at Constantinople they indulged in an orgy of burning and looting that greatly displeased the Byzantine emperor, who promptly sent them on their way to do battle with the Turks. This resulted in the final catastrophe for the People's Crusade, which ended with the death or enslavement of most of these first Crusaders.

Meanwhile, back in Europe, more sober-headed leaders were preparing for a much more organized type of warfare. Four major armies were slowly organized. The first one was commanded by the Duke of Lower Lorraine, Godfrey de Bouillon, and his

Plate 1

Stone Trilithons of Stonehenge
(Photograph by Gilbert Spesock).

Plate 2

Charlemagne's cathedral at Aachen
(Photograph by Stefan Brenner).

Plate 3

The Tour Magdala constructed by Berenger Sauniere at
Rennes-le-Chateau. Was it used to view astronomical alignments
of surrounding churches and landmarks?
(Photograph by Martha Neyman).

Plate 4

Ruins of the Templar Castle on the peak of Bezu
(Photograph by Martha Neyman).

Plate 5

Church at Rennes-le-Chateau
(Photograph by Martha Neyman).

Plate 6

Cathedral at Santiago de Compostela
(Photograph by Martha Neyman).

Plate 7

Sunset at the end of Pennsylvania Avenue on August 10. At this point, later in the day, the star Regulus will also set, marking the location of a stellar right triangle that is commemorated by the Federal Triangle.

Plate 8

The Assumption of the Virgin by Nicholas Poussin.

Plate 9

Plate 9: Masonic Temple in Alexandria, Virginia.

Plate 10

Plate 10: Astronomically oriented colonial church—Christ Church—constructed in Virginia in 1735.

brother, Baldwin. Two other armies were headed by other French noblemen, and a fourth was led by Robert of Normandy, the son of William the Conqueror, who only thirty years previously, in 1066, had crossed the English Channel to attack England and establish a Norman kingdom to rule the country. All of these experienced warriors were expected to fare much better in battle than the People's Crusade.

These armies left France by various routes in August 1096 and finally arrived in Constantinople by winter of the same year. After staying the winter in this glorious Byzantine city, the armies assembled for battle and attacked the Turkish city of Nicea and eventually conquered it by June of 1097.

The next target, the imposing walled city of Antioch, proved to be a much greater challenge. Even the path to Antioch was difficult, leading through a dry, uninhabited region of the Anatolian plateau with no food and little water, causing considerable suffering for the Crusaders and death of many horses from thirst (Howarth, 1982, p. 36). When the Crusaders finally arrived at Antioch, they were confronted with an extensive system of walls surrounding the city dotted with 400 towers that guarded all approaches and gates. The Crusaders were forced to lay siege to the city for ten weeks and also to do battle with a large column of Turkish soldiers that Duqaq of Damascus had sent to relieve Antioch. Finally, Antioch was subdued through an act of treachery: Crusader forces bribed a gatekeeper, who let the enemy into the city before dawn and thereby broke the defenses of Antioch.

Crusader forces rested and regrouped for five months following the fall of Antioch, and then poised themselves for the final attack upon Jerusalem. Jerusalem itself also had the potential for considerable resistance. Its governor, Iftikhar ad-Daula, had poisoned the wells surrounding Jerusalem to deny the Crusaders water in the thirsty land, and had expelled thousands of Christians with possible sympathies for the Crusaders from the city. In addition, a rescuing Egyptian army commanded by a general named al-Afdal was on the march (Payne, 2000, p. 109). However, Crusaders reached Jerusalem in June of 1099 and after five weeks of siege, managed to connect a siege tower to some wooden battlements of the wall surrounding Jerusalem. Immediately streams of knights, headed by Godfrey de Bouillon, passed over the wall and entered the city.

The victorious army went on a rampage inside Jerusalem, slaughtering the inhabitants until the streets ran with blood. At least 70,000 inhabitants were killed and mosques and churches were ransacked for loot. Gold and silver treasures were looted from the Dome of the Rock. Muslims who had taken a last stand at the al-Aqsa Mosque were put to death. Jews, the people of Jesus, were not spared: Those who had sought refuge in the chief synagogue were killed when it was set on fire by Crusaders (Payne, 2000, p. 102). After dispatching their victims, the Crusaders converged on the Church of the Holy Sepulcher to celebrate mass in honor of their victory. Within several days, a council of the conquerors met and awarded control of the city to Godfrey de Bouillon.

The ancestry of Godfrey de Bouillon has been examined in detail by Henry Lincoln, who has arrived at some rather startling conclusions. The ancestors of Godfrey appear to have originated in a portion of southeast France around Narbonne, not far from the location of Rennes-le-Chateau. This area had an unusually large Jewish community that had arisen in ages past, apparently due to emigration from Spain and even the Holy Land. One nobleman of the area, an illustrious associate of Charlemagne named Guillem de Gellome, was a descendent of this Jewish community and used the Jewish symbol of the Lion of Judah in his heraldry. In A.D. 792, Guillem established a respected library and center for Judaic studies in southern France. One of his descendents, Hugues de Plantard, was the great-grandfather of Godfrey de Bouillon. So in a certain sense, the recovery of Jerusalem by Godfrey was a reconfirmation of his Jewish origins (Baigent, 1996, p. 421).

The rule of Jerusalem by Godfrey de Bouillon lasted only one year—he died in 1100. Upon his death, his brother Baldwin was crowned the first Latin King of Jerusalem. It was due to the persistence and military abilities of Baldwin I that the struggling Christian kingdom was able to survive its first years and even expand to include the ports of Acre and Caesarea, which were vitally needed to transport more goods and fighting men from faraway Europe (Howarth, 1982, p. 41).

The Creation of the Knights Templar

The death of Baldwin I in 1118 marks the beginning of the story of the Knights Templar. Baldwin I was succeeded by his cousin, who became King Baldwin II. On his accession to the throne, he was approached by a group of nine knights, who asked his approval for the creation of a new order of knights to be called the Poor Fellow Soldiers of Jesus Christ or the Poor Knights of Christ. Ostensibly, the purpose of the new Order of Knights was to secure the safety of pilgrims coming to the Holy Land.

The leaders of this proposed order, as far as can be discerned from sketchy historical records written years later by Guillaume de Tyre, were a French knight, Hugh de Payens, who had been on crusade in the Middle East for twenty-two years, and another French knight, Andre de Montbard. King Baldwin II was happy to accept this proposal, and gave the knights quarters in a building on the supposed site of the Temple of Jerusalem. It is from this location that the Order soon became known as the Knights of the Temple of Solomon, or Knights Templar.

The Order that these and seven other companions proposed to initiate was a strict and highly religious one, with numerous rules and regulations. All knights were sworn to obedience, chastity, and poverty. Knights Templar were forbidden to cut their beards and were obliged to wear an outer garment or cloak that specifically was to be white in color. They were allowed to eat meat no more than three times a week, sleep on straw mattresses, and have no decorations on their clothing. As the Knights Templar became more successful and widespread, all worldly possessions of each applicant were required to be donated to the Order.

This disciplined life, imposed upon every Templar, stands in sharp contrast to the values of the modern world, in which the most highly promoted features of life are the acquisition of wealth and comfort, the fulfillment of sexual pleasure, and the attainment of as much freedom and independence of thought as possible. From our modern perspective, it is difficult to understand what inspired wealthy, powerful men to join such an order. Even in an era when poor peasants were convinced to risk their lives to conquer the Holy Land, the sacrifice entailed in joining the Knights Templar stands out. It is tempting to wonder if the Templars did indeed have some extraordinary means of motivating potential applicants in the form of some unusual relic or religious information. As will be discussed later, there is evidence that the Templars later possessed the Holy Relic now known as the Shroud of Turin. Whatever the explanation, as the Templar organization matured, it became one of the most successful institutions of the Middle Ages.

Not long after the Templars became established in Jerusalem, its founders returned to Europe to request aid in the form of both manpower and material. Andre de Montbard returned to northern France in 1126 to visit his nephew, the famous cleric Bernard, Abbot of the Monastery of Clairvaux, later to be named St. Bernard. The widely admired Bernard appealed to many to assist the Templars. New and associate members of the Order were acquired, and they granted the Templars land and treasure. One of the first donors was Count Thybaud of Champagne, who donated property to the Templars in 1127 (Howarth, 1982, p. 64). Bernard wrote to Pope Honorius II, who responded by ordering the convening of a council to further the growth of the Order.

The first Grand Master of the Templars, Hugh de Payens, also traveled from the Holy Land to attend this council in Troyes, France in 1127. The council, in consultation with Payens and Bernard, established all the rules of the Order and created a formal ceremony for applicants, which demanded that all applicants be "a servant and slave of the Order for life," never marry, and obey all the rules (Howarth, 1982, p. 60). Following the council at Troyes, Hugh crossed the Channel to England and met with King Henry I, who welcomed him warmly and gave additional donations of gold and silver to the cause. Hugh's tour of England was a tremendous success, and inspired additional lavish donations of property in Buckinghamshire, Lincolnshire, Hertfordshire, and Essex to the Templars (Howarth, 1982, p. 68). In England alone, the Templars acquired 74 major properties and titles to numerous smaller villages, priories, and churches (Baigent, 1989, p. 46). The Templars rapidly developed into a wealthy and very influential organization.

Once again, as Henry Lincoln has pointed out, one can wonder at the propitious timing of all these events. Within eight years of the founding of the Order, massive donations of wealth and property were flowing in. Was this just a coincidence, or evidence of some preexisting coordination of events that guaranteed a source of funds? If the Templars had been founded exclusively to protect pilgrims, why was the Order created as long as eighteen years after the conquest of Jerusalem? Why not establish the Order right away? Perhaps one answer is that the creation of a network of influential European personalities who guaranteed sources of income did not take effect until 1118. The motivations and goals of these closely related leaders may have been more complicated than the mere protection of pilgrims journeying to the Holy Land.

Regardless of the underlying reasons, history records that the Templars rapidly became a success story. Hugh de Payens reportedly brought 300 new recruits back to the Holy Land when he returned to Jerusalem (Howarth, 1982, p. 70). The fighting ability of the Templars and the security of their numerous castles, spread throughout Europe from the Holy Land to England, allowed for the function of an early, rudimentary "banking" system, in which a promissory note issued by Templars in England would be honored by other Templars in distant lands (Robinson, 1989, p. 75). Templars occupied positions of honor and influence rivaled only by the royal houses of Europe. Perhaps the most noteworthy gift to the Templars was the decree, granted by Pope Innocent II in 1139, that the Templars could build their own churches, police their own knights, be free of taxation or tithes from any other religious group, and be subject to no authority except for the Pope's own (Howarth, 1982, p. 80).

Many of the knights first inducted into the Knights Templar came from noble houses located near Rennes-le-Chateau. For example, the fourth Grand Master of the Templars, Bertrand of

Blanchefort, constructed the Blanchefort castle located several miles to the east of Rennes-le-Chateau (see fig. 11, p. 62) (Baigent, 1996, p. 25). This Templar castle occupies a key point in the pentagonal scheme of geometric alignments of the structures surrounding Rennes-le-Chateau. As we shall see, many of the sites discussed in this book contain stone buildings or monuments constructed by Templars. For example, a Templar gravesite is located near Charlemagne's cathedral at Aachen, as noted above.

Templars have long been rumored to have possessed some type of secret knowledge, perhaps because of events surrounding their demise. The question of whether or not the Templars did adhere to some heretical principles or instead were just labeled as heretics after their demise has long been debated (see Partner, 1981 for a lengthy discussion of this debate). Curiously, the Rule of the Order adopted in France commanded Templars to go to places where excommunicated knights were assembled and to recruit any excommunicates willing to enter the Order (Howarth, 1982, p. 83). This very unusual, and secret, mandate to French Templars, which is in complete violation of Church rules for society, does suggest some tolerance for unorthodox religious thought on the part of the Templars. It is likely that many persecuted Cathars found a haven in the Templar organization, and that their religious ideas could have had some influence within the Templars. Perhaps a knowledge of ancient, sacred geometry of sites in Europe could also have been part of Templar lore.

The Decline of the Crusader Kingdom

As their hold on Jerusalem and neighboring territories appeared to solidify, the original unity of the Crusaders began to come apart. A feud erupted between the Frankish rulers of Antioch and the city of Edessa, and the ruler of Edessa moved his army from the city to meet the challenge from his fellow Crusader. This rash move was taken advantage of by Prince Zengi of Syria, who attacked and conquered the city in 1144 and massacred all European Christians within it (Payne, 200, p. 150). News of this disaster provoked tremendous shock in Europe and immediate calls for another Crusade. On Easter Sunday in 1146, at Vezelay, not far from Paris, Bernard of Clairveaux spoke to an enormous crowd and urged them to go on Crusade. As had happened before with Urban II, Bernard was overwhelmed with the enthusiasm of the crowd and planning for the new military venture commenced. Within a year, Bernard, the Pope, and King Louis VII of France, together with three hundred Knights Templar garbed in white, stood at the head of a new Second Crusade that left France for the Holy Land (Howarth, 1982, p. 85). The French army was eventually joined in the Holy Land by a German army led by King Conrad III.

The German army met the opposing Turks first, and came to a disastrous end. German soldiers, exhausted from a long march across Turkey, were attacked by fresh Turkish troops who routed them and killed or captured three quarters of the German army. The French army, following in the traces of the German army, also experienced numerous disastrous battles, including an unwise and unsuccessful attack upon Damascus. Finally, by 1149, both Kings had returned to Europe by sea, effectively ending the Second Crusade.

Despite these failures, the Frankish Kingdom of Jerusalem held onto its territory for decades more. The only real threat to the security of the Kingdom did not arise until 1169, when Saladin seized power in Cairo.

Saladin was one of the most fascinating personalities in the history of the Middle Ages. He was of Kurdish ancestry and was born Yusuf ibn Ayyub (Joseph, son of Job) in what is now Tikrit, Iraq (yes, also the hometown of Saddam Hussein). As an adult, he took the name Salah al-Din ("rectifier of the Faith"). His uncle Shirkuh became vizier of Egypt in 1169; upon his death, Saladin took over this position and gained control of Egypt, and through warfare and diplomacy brought Egypt into harmony with the government of Syria (Payne, 2000, p. 191).

This was a fatal development for the Crusaders, for now they were surrounded on two sides by Muslim forces that co-operated with each other. Previously, joint action by Syria and Egypt had been impossible, since these countries were dominated by two different and hostile divisions of Islam: Sunni (Egypt) and Shiite (Syria) sects. This division of Islam arose because of disagreement about how the leader of the Muslim community (the caliph) should be chosen. The Sunni sect (from the Arabic for "path") represents the so-called followers of the path, who believed the caliph should be elected or appointed.

The Shi'a sect (from the Arabic for "party of 'Ali"; Ali was the son-in-law of Muhammad) believed the caliph should be chosen from the close relatives of Muhammad. Each sect regarded the other as representing non-believers. But by 1169, these differences were eliminated by Saladin, and the forces of Syria and Egypt were united.

Saladin initially tried to capture the southernmost fort of the Kingdom of Jerusalem in 1170, but was rebuffed by a force of Templars and signed a truce. In 1180, however, this truce was rashly broken by a Frankish prince, Reynald of Chatillon, who led a raiding party of about 600 men upon the Holy Muslim cities of Mecca and Medina in Arabia. This outrage infuriated Saladin, who vowed to capture and kill Reynald and conquer the Christian Kingdom of Jerusalem.

Saladin required years to accomplish this goal. He was aided by constant squabbling and infighting among the Crusader ranks. After a number of attempts to take either Jerusalem or the castle of his enemy, Reynald, Saladin finally faced the Crusader army in 1187 near two hills called the Horns of Hattin, near the Sea of Galilee. Ironically, according to some traditions, this had been the site of Christ's Sermon on the Mount (Howarth, 1982, p. 153). Saladin surrounded the Frankish forces with swarms of archers and decimated the Christian army. Reynald was captured and personally executed by Saladin. All Knights Templar who had participated in the battle were executed with swords wielded by mullahs and religious teachers (Payne, 2000, p. 208).

With the main Christian force defeated, it was only a few more months before Jerusalem was also attacked. Initially, Saladin tried to breach the walls of the city using siege engines, but the desperate Christian defenders raced out of the city and quickly destroyed them. The man in charge of the defense of Jerusalem, Balian of Ibelin, parlayed with Saladin in an attempt to avoid great loss of life. Realizing that his position was weak, Balian nevertheless averred that the defenders would fight to the death if need be, taking with them thousands of Muslims still living in the city and destroying Muslim holy places like the Al-Aqsa mosque. Saladin responded by saying he would accept the peaceful surrender of the city if a general ransom were paid from the treasure that had been donated by Henry II of England (Payne, 2000, p. 210). All Christians leaving the city were searched for valuables as they passed through the city gates. Saladin ordered that all traces of the Templars be removed from their headquarters, which possessed a huge hall decorated with trophies of war and a stable big enough to accommodate 2,000 horses. Jerusalem would never again be the home of the Knights of the Temple of Solomon.

News of this fresh disaster reached England three months later. Richard I, son of King Henry II and later to be known as Richard the Lion Hearted, reacted by immediately declaring that he was taking the Cross. His father the King also was convinced and started making preparations for a Third Crusade to recover Jerusalem. He was not to live to see this event, however, since he fell ill and died, leaving the task and his kingdom to his successor,

Richard. Richard responded with a vigorous campaign to squeeze as much revenue from England as possible: He sold offices and titles to the highest bidders and eventually was able to pay for thousands of horses and a fleet of 250 ships that was directed to France. By 1190, he had joined forces with King Phillip II of France to assemble a host of 100,000 men, which made its way via several routes to the Holy Land.

In spite of valiant efforts, this Third Crusade failed to recover Jerusalem, and was terminated by a peace treaty with Saladin in 1192. It was succeeded by the Fourth Crusade, the pathetic Children's Crusade of 1212, which resulted in the enslavement of thousands of children, and by Crusades Five through Eight. None of these Crusades were effective; the last Christian city in the Holy Land, Acre, surrendered in 1291. The gold and silver treasure from the Temple at Acre was evacuated to Cyprus along with a few survivors. The era of the Crusaders in the Holy Land was over.

The Final Years of the Knights Templar

Templars expelled from the Holy Land at least had the consolation that their remaining brethren in Europe would welcome them to their numerous properties. In France alone, at least 150 farms and manors were owned by Templars (Howarth, 1982, p. 234). But the lifestyle in Europe was totally different from the one the Crusaders had become accustomed to in Palestine: European Templars were more preoccupied with farming, money lending, and commerce than with warfare. In England, as in other countries, the Templars were not only uniquely exempt from taxation, but also served as tax collectors for the Crown and money lenders to the King. They were allowed to charge a fee for money lending—not formally as "interest," since that would have violated Church rules against usury, but ostensibly to cover the time, trouble, and risks of money lending. All in all, the Templars continued to prosper in Europe, accumulating a reputed 9,000 properties throughout the continent and in the British Isles (Howarth, 1982, p. 246).

The 200-year period of glory for the Templars came to an end in 1307 due to the machinations of a supremely ambitious and unscrupulous man. This man, King Phillip IV, accomplished a variety of unsavory things in his lifetime. Perhaps the root cause of all his actions was an insatiable appetite for money (Howarth, 1982, p. 254). In the 1290s Phillip devalued his own currency time and time again to bring in more revenue, causing the coinage to lose two-thirds of its value in ten years. He even imposed taxes upon Church properties to bring in more money, which was unheard of at the time. This brought him into serious conflict with Pope Boniface VIII, who forbid him from taxing the clergy in 1296. Phillip responded by prohibiting the export of gold from France to the Vatican. The conflict between the two men escalated until, in 1303, the Estates General of France accused Boniface of sodomy, sorcery, and heresy—charges that would later be directed against the Templars. Boniface then threatened to excommunicate the entire nation of France.

Anxious to avoid this catastrophe, Phillip decided upon an audacious plan: Before Boniface could act, he would have him kidnapped! Phillip entrusted this task to a loyal crony, William de Nogaret, who had cause to despise the Papacy. Nogaret's parents had been Cathars and had been burned alive as heretics. Nogaret's plans for kidnapping the Pope proved successful, but the shock of imprisonment for the eighty-six-year-old pontiff proved too great, and Boniface died after one month in captivity. Boniface's successor, Benedict XI, also posed a threat to Phillip, but not for long: Benedict died mysteriously only eight months after assuming the Papacy. Many suspected Phillip of having him poisoned.

Not long after these events, Phillip applied for membership into the Knights Templar. The Templars refused. The reasons were never stated, cloaked in the secrecy of the Order, but one can imagine that the membership might have been extremely wary of becoming dominated by the powerful and unscrupulous Phillip. Phillip was to prove a dangerous enemy of the Templars (Howarth, 1982, p. 259).

Several years after his rejection by the Templars, Phillip had the humiliating experience of depending on them for his safety. Another of his monetary schemes provoked such anger in Paris that Phillip fled to the Paris Temple to save himself from rioting mobs. He had ample time to inspect the obvious signs of wealth and power that the Temple symbolized: The Paris Temple complex was surrounded by a wall eighteen feet high, could accommodate 300 knights and their horses and retainers, and included a tower 160 feet high that could be seen throughout Paris (Howarth, 1982, p. 262).

After his stay with the Templars, Phillip solved his problems with the Papacy in a characteristic manner. By "packing" the Church Council with a majority of French bishops, he stage-managed the election of a "puppet" Pope, the archbishop of Bordeaux, who became Clement V. Clement was an understandably frightened and obedient servant of Phillip IV. He had the Papacy removed from Rome to the French site at Avignon, causing untold confusion and conflict within the Christian world. More importantly, he colluded with Phillip in the destruction of the Knights Templar.

In 1306, Pope Clement sent a letter to the Master of the Temple, Jacques de Molay, requesting that he journey from Cyprus to Rome to supposedly consult with him about the possibility of a new Crusade. Molay, who had participated in the final defense of Acre and who had been elected Master thirteen years previously, assented and came home to France. When he met with Clement, he was astonished and horrified to hear that Phillip had made accusations of heresy and treason against the Templars. De Molay denied the validity of the charges, and Clement himself tried to avert any further conflict or inquiries. All was in vain, however, for onOctober 13, 1307, Phillip II ordered all 5,000 Knights Templar in France arrested on charges of heresy. The entire operation was masterminded by de Nogaret, the former Cathar who had kidnapped the Pope for Phillip.

Throughout France, the Templars were rounded up and imprisoned; their possessions were seized, and they were put on trial.

Soon, confessions of heresy by Templars, obtained under the influence of torture, were produced. The accusations, supported by
confessions, declared that the Templars spat upon images of Christ,
indulged in homosexual orgies, and worshipped an idol in the
shape of a human head. Hugh de Pairaud, Treasurer of the Temple,
confessed that he had "seen, held, and stroked an idol shaped like
a human head...which brought the Templars all their worldly
power and wealth" (Howarth, 1982, p. 280).

Henry Lincoln and Michael Baigent note that when a Templar
building in Paris was searched, a silver reliquary in the shape of a
woman's head was found that allegedly contained portions of a
skeleton and skull, wrapped in white linen. These bore a label on
which was written "CAPUT LVIII," followed by the astronomical sign for the constellation Virgo (Baigent, 1996, p. 81).

Is it possible that the Templars had convinced themselves that
they possessed a uniquely holy relic, a portion of the mortal remains of the Virgin Mary? As will be discussed later in this book,
there is evidence that the Templars possessed the Shroud of Turin,
long regarded as the burial cloth of Christ. So it is conceivable
that such a relic could have been a source of the extraordinary
inspiration needed to sustain the sacrifices and discipline of the
Templars. Even the existence of such a relic, of course, is
highly questionable, and is in direct conflict with the orthodox
position of the Church that Mary ascended directly into heaven.

Why, however, would a Christian reliquary described by Lincoln and Baigent be labeled with the non-Christian sign for the

constellation Virgo? This theme is of interest to us in the context of the arrangement of castles and churches at Rennes-le-Chateau, which point to the sun rising in the constellation Virgo on August 15, the day of the Ascension of the Virgin into heaven, as discussed in Ch. 3. Perhaps this reliquary is evidence that the Templars mystically revered both the Virgin Mary and the Virgo constellation.

The campaign against the Templars seemed to be headed for a speedy conclusion satisfactory to Phillip when an unexpected obstacle arose. The previously docile Clement V gathered up his courage and wrote a letter to Phillip denying him the right to arrest the Templars and noting that they had traditionally been accountable only to the Papacy. Moreover, Clement encouraged an independent investigation of the Templars by clerical bodies and not by Phillip's henchmen. As a result, 60 confessions, including de Molay's, were withdrawn and denied by accused Templars, leading to hope that the Templars might escape the fate that Phillip had prepared for them. As a result of all this controversy, Templars in England were not even arrested until 1308, and were treated tolerantly. No English Templar ever confessed to any sort of wrongdoing.

But hope proved to be in vain. Phillip applied a campaign of slander and pressure to Clement V, accusing him of taking bribes from the Templars, and presented him with more tortured Templars who reaffirmed the accusations of heresy and wrongdoing. For a time, in 1310, the Templars were tried by a papal commission that promised to hear the testimony of some 600 Templars who claimed to be innocent. But Phillip had arranged for a separate prosecution of other Templars at the same time, headed by an archbishop he had appointed, and this prosecution sentenced fifty-four Templars to be burned alive as heretics. When the sentence was carried out, fear broke the resistance of the remaining Templars, many of whom preferred to confess and face prison rather than be burned at the stake. Under continual pressure from Phillip, Clement V finally dissolved the Order in 1311 and declared that Templar property belonged to their longtime rivals, the Knights Hospitallers (Howarth, 1982, p. 305; Robinson, 1989, pp. 17–36). Two of the last victims of the trial were the elderly Grand Master, Jacques de Molay, and the Preceptor of Normandy, Geoffrey de Charnay, who were burned at the stake in 1314 (Baigent, 1996, p. 73).

Lincoln and others have maintained that while the official organization of the Knights Templar vanished during these tragic years, an underground society persisted, devoted to the defense of its former members and determined to resist the tyranny of King and Church. One organization that might have inherited these goals, surprisingly enough, might be that of the Freemasons.

✴

CHAPTER 6

Successors of the Knights Templar

Freemasonry

Freemasonry, as it exists today, appears to represent no more than a collection of like-minded men and women who periodically meet to socialize, philosophize, and to perform charitable acts in their communities. Masonic lodges are found throughout the world. The Freemasons of America can claim a total membership of almost two million members; they seem no more mysterious than other types of clubs and organizations. This modern-day acceptance of Freemasonry is, however, quite different from perceptions of Freemasonry in the past, when it was considered a dangerous and frightening "secret society." What are the origins, goals, and secrets of Freemasonry? Do they relate in any way to the Templars or to an interest in the spiritual significance of astronomical events?

The existence of a secret society of Freemasons was first revealed in 1717, when the first Grand Lodge of Masons in London made its existence known to the public (Baigent, 1989, p. 174). However, published works establish that this society had existed for some considerable time before that. For example, the scholar and antiquarian Elias Ashmole, who founded the Ashmolean Museum at Oxford, is known to have been inducted into Freemasonry in 1646, and a poem by Henry Adamson, written in 1638, refers to Masons (Baigent, 1989, p. 156). A manuscript published in 1650 called the "Chymical Collections" shows clear illustrations of Masonic symbols, including dual columns and the sun and the moon (McNulty, 1991, p. 69). A document written by William Schaw in 1600 also establishes an early date for Freemasonry (Knight, 1997, p. 330). Thus, it is widely acknowledged that the Masonic organizations can be traced back at least to the beginning of the seventeenth century.

Freemasonry has a documented history in the United States that goes back nearly as far as that of England. The first Grand Lodge in the Western Hemisphere was established in Boston in 1733, headed by a prosperous merchant named Henry Price and assisted by one Andrew Belched, son of the colonial governor of Massachusetts. Benjamin Franklin, a Mason, attended a meeting at this lodge in 1743, as did Paul Revere in 1760 (Schmidt, 1980, p. 121). As will be discussed later, many revolutionaries who founded the United States were inspired by Masonic ideals of brotherhood and freedom.

Many researchers have sought to expand our meager knowledge of the origins of Freemasonry. Obviously, the elaborate ceremonies and symbolism of Freemasonry could not have originated overnight in the early 1700s, when the first Lodges were publicly acknowledged. But how far back can the history of Masonry be traced?

A number of documents were published in the early 1800s that claimed to present evidence for an early history of Masonry. For example, in 1815, Mr. James Dowland published a manuscript that he claimed was the transcription of an old parchment he had discovered that detailed the founding mythology of Masonry. This original parchment was never made available to the public and cannot be located today; however, the old fashioned words, spelling, and writing style of Dowland's transcription of the alleged parchment belong to the middle of the sixteenth century. This document, in brief, spelled out the seven learned disciplines most esteemed by Freemasonry—grammar, rhetoric, dialectic, arithmetic, geometry, music, and astronomy—and stated that Masonry originated in the time of the Old Testament and was connected with the building of the Temple of Solomon (Mackey, 1996, p. 15). These and similar manuscripts published in the 1800s constitute the so-called Legend of the Craft. Most of these documents portray Solomon as the first Grand Master of Masonry and state that he was very learned in geometry and astronomy/astrology (Mackey, 1996, p. 81). Another prominent source of Masonic lore was the claim, by Chevalier Michael Ramsay in 1740, that many of the traditions of Masonry arose during the Crusades and were connected to the Knights Templar. Ramsay had an early and prominent position in European Freemasonry and initiated the custom of many, higher levels of the Masonic Order (Mackey, 1996, p. 245). The archaic wording of these documents, if they were real, does suggest that some sort of Masonic organization may have been present several centuries before the public declaration of Masonry in 1717. But these Legends, some of which are preposterous, can in no way be interpreted as a serious historical record of Freemasonry.

Some even older traces of Freemasonry, which also show a connection between the Templars and the Masons, are apparent on ancient gravestones (Fig. 13). For example, a gravestone at the Templar castle at Athlit, Israel, dating from A.D. 1291, bears a familiar symbol of Freemasonry, the architect's tool called a set-square. Also, another Templar gravestone at Loch Sween in Scotland bears a similar inscription (Baigent, 1989, p. 10). Possibly, some of the symbolism and philosophy of the Masons could have originated with the Templars. What do we know about the symbolism and philosophy of Freemasonry?

While some aspects of Freemasonry are still withheld from the general public, the broad outlines of Masonic thinking and symbolism have long been freely published and generally known and have been summarized in an excellent book by W. Kirk McNulty (1991). The basic requirement for entry into the organization, at least in North America and the United Kingdom, is a belief in a supreme Deity; however, a belief in a Christian God is not specified, and indeed, Freemasonry has encouraged people of diverse

Fig. 13

Masonic Tracing Board

faiths (Muslims, Jews, and Buddhists, for example) to join. This religious tolerance, unusual for the times in which Freemasonry originated, may have developed during the centuries of Templar experience among the "infidels" of the Middle East.

Freemasonry in Europe has traditionally differed substantially from that of the new world, having a more revolutionary and anti-clerical orientation; the Grand Orient of France admits atheists, though does not declare itself an officially atheistic organzation (Schmidt, 1980, p. 120). This anti-religious attitude of Continental Masonry provoked Pope Clement XII to issue a Papal Bull in 1738 condemning Masonry and forbidding Catholics to join. However, the position of the Church has softened considerably since then, and in 1976 Freemasonry was taken off the list of proscribed organizations, so that Catholics are now permitted membership (Schmidt, 1980, p. 130).

An applicant wishing to join the Masons must pass through three qualifying stages, or "degrees," which are each accompanied by a ritual of passage. An applicant of the First Degree is called an Entered Apprentice, who progresses to the Second Degree of Fellow Craftsman, and finally completes the Third Degree of Master Mason, generally within a year. At each stage of preparation, an applicant is required to master a defined set of symbols and instructions of Freemasonry and to take part in a ceremony. Each ceremony has its own special features. To qualify as an Entered Apprentice, an applicant must wear a ceremonial linen garment. His left sleeve is rolled up, a hood is placed over his head (he is "hoodwinked"), and a rope or noose called a "cable tow" is placed around his neck. The cable tow is symbolically supposed to guide and control the applicant. An applicant is also required to roll up one pant leg and to wear a slipper on that foot. Slight variations of this ceremony are applied to the next two degrees of initiation. The exact meaning or symbolism of all of these actions is not explicitly spelled out in Masonic literature and may represent a tradition that is not completely understood by most Masons (Schmidt, 1980, p. 123; Knight, 1997, p. 3).

To assist applicants undergoing these ceremonies of initiation, the symbolism of Freemasonry is summarized and presented on paintings called Tracing Boards. All Tracing Boards present the three fundamental symbols of Masonry: 1) a volume of Sacred Law; 2) a set-square of the type used by carpenters to draw a right angle; and 3) a compass used for measuring angles and drawing circles. These symbols, which seem clearly connected to geometry and architecture, are supposed to represent Divinity, the Psyche, and the Spirit, respectively. Before an applicant can successfully complete these initiation rites, he must swear an obligation that he will not reveal Masonic secrets "under no less penalty than to have my throat cut across, my tongue torn out by the roots, and my body buried in the rough sands of the sea at low water mark" (Schmidt, 1980, p. 123). The penalty is entirely symbolic here, as it is never actually applied.

The symbols that are first introduced on a First Degree Tracing Board bear a distinct relationship to astronomy. These include a blazing star, or Glory, which is supposed to represent the Divine Universe; a depiction of the sun; and a depiction of the moon, sometimes accompanied by seven stars that symbolize the moving bodies or planets, as opposed to fixed stars, that were known at the time in astronomy (e.g. Mercury, Venus, Moon, Earth, Mars, Jupiter, and Saturn). The sun and moon represent a Masonic principle of Duality, since many of their qualities are opposites: The sun is a brilliant, hot, unchanging celestial body, whereas the moon is a pale, cool, and changeable (with numerous phases) object. Nevertheless, they appear to be almost exactly the same size, which allows the moon to precisely cover the solar disc during eclipses. Nowadays, we regard the similarity in apparent size of the moon and sun to be merely a coincidence, but the ancients long regarded this as evidence of celestial order and harmony.

Few other religious or philosophical organizations existing today show this persistent fascination with the moon and sun, which is reminiscent of the meticulous solar and lunar alignments of the megalithic monuments we have already discussed. Is this astronomical theme in Freemasonry a coincidence, or was it inherited from the Templars and from even earlier societies?

Other Masonic symbols that accompany the sun and moon are a Corinthian column, which represents an active, creative spirit, and a Doric column, representing a passive, reflective mode of thinking (McNulty, 1991, p. 18). In some paintings, a third Ionic column is portrayed that is supposed to balance and mediate between the other two columns. The two main columns are supposed to have originated in the Temple of Solomon and were named Jachin and Boaz, referring to the names of the high priest at the Temple of Solomon and the great-grandfather of David the King, respectively (Knight, 1997, p. 7). These symbols appear to have a very old history: Pillars inscribed with these Masonic names, dating from A.D. 1042, are present in the cathedral of Wurzburg (Ovason, 2000, p. 91).

In Tracing Boards of the Second Degree, the two Masonic columns can be portrayed as composed of brass, and are said to be hollow and to contain the accumulated archives of the Craft (McNulty, 1991, p. 24). This relates to the claim by Abbe Sauniere that secret manuscripts were found within a hollow column in the church at Rennes-le-Chateau (see Chapter 4): Any Mason hearing such a description would have immediately recognized the potentially strong connection with Freemasonry. These symbols also show another connection between the Temple of Solomon, the Knights Templar, and the Freemasons.

Another feature of the Tracing Boards is a frequent depiction of a winding staircase or a Jacob's Ladder ascending to heaven. Each staircase often contains three principal steps or rungs, representing faith (for the first degree Entered Apprentice), hope (for the second degree Fellow Craftsman), and charity (for the third degree Master Mason who has achieved his goals).

Each Masonic lodge is presided over by a Master, assisted by six other officers, who guide the rituals and ceremonies involved in the initiation of new applicants. The lowest ranking officer is the Tyler, who plays the role of an outer guard. The Tyler is equipped with a ceremonial sword and is responsible for keeping uninitiated persons ("cowens" and eavesdroppers) away from the Lodge. The Tyler is also associated with a basic science, that of grammar. The other six officers are the inner guard, the junior deacon, the senior deacon, the junior warden, the senior warden, and the worshipful master.

More evidence can be found for a preoccupation with astronomy in Freemasonry. For example, in the layout of a Masonic Lodge, the sun and moon are always represented by two of three lighted candles placed near the altar, the third candle representing the Master. The official jewel of the senior deacon depicts the sun, whereas the jewel of the junior deacon depicts the moon. Some early Masonic lodges were called "Full Moon Lodges" because they met only on the Fridays preceding the full moon. The two principal festival days for Masons are called the Saints John days and are dedicated to the two patron saints of Masonry, John the Baptist (day of June 24) and John the Evangelist (day of December 27). It is probably not a coincidence that these two days fall very close to the summer and winter solstices, respectively (Herner, 1984, p. 31). Finally, a new applicant in Freemasonry is often likened to a growing sprig of corn. In turn, the sprig of corn is often related to the star Spica in the constellation of Virgo (Ovason, 2000, pp. 99-102).

The ceremony attendant to the Third Degree, conveying an applicant to the rank of Master Mason, is perhaps the most striking and peculiar portion of Freemasonry. This ceremony recreates the supposed murder, by three conspirators, of the principal architect of the Temple of Solomon, named Hiram Abif. Hiram Abif was the son of a widow lady, and was sent by King Hiram of Tyre, who lent Solomon wooden beams and craftsmen to help him complete the Temple of Solomon (Mackey, 1996, p. 76). Though no harm comes to an initiate, he does mimic the death of Hiram Abif and receives three ceremonial blows to the head. This ceremony is supposed to represent the spiritual death and rebirth of the applicant into the Craft. Appropriately enough, a Tracing Board of the Third Degree shows symbols such as a coffin and a skull above two crossed thighbones, i.e., skull and crossbones.

The origin of the Hiram Abif character in the rites of Masonry is obscure; no real historical figure exactly corresponding to Hiram Abif has been identified with certainty. Several authors have proposed that the Hiram Abif character originates in historical events in ancient Egypt (Knight, 1997, p. 134). The twelve conspirators who had plotted to kill him in Masonic tradition but then recant, represent the twelve signs of the Zodiac. Hiram Abif is "killed" in ceremonies, at the east door of a Lodge, by the three other conspirators who persist. Hiram is raised up again by a Master using the secret "lion's grip," which may correspond to the sign of Leo, at which the midsummer sun regains its full strength (Heckethorn, 1965, p. 27). Obviously, a number of symbolic or historical explanations may apply to the character of Hiram Abif. The seven officers (including the Master) who participate in initiation rites may correspond in number to the seven planets recognized in antiquity (Sun, Moon, Mercury, Venus, Mars, Jupiter, and Saturn).

The skull and crossbones symbol used in the Third Degree apparently originated with the Templars, and may have been displayed on the battle flag flown on Templar sailing ships (Baigent, 1996, p. 84; Knight, 1997, p. 76 and 316). How this emblem came to be flown on pirate ships several centuries after the demise of the Templars is not known. Also, the scholastic secret society "Skull and Bones," founded at Yale more than a century ago, shows a clear connection with these symbols of Freemasonry. Is there any way of determining where these peculiar themes came from?

The author John Robinson has cast doubt upon the traditional explanation for the origin of the Freemasons, namely that they originated from a stonecutting guild of masons. In spite of careful effort, he has been unable to confirm any written records of any such guild in any locale in England (Robinson, 1989, p. 199). In contrast, many of the peculiar words found in Masonic ceremonies appear to have been derived from medieval French. For example, puzzling words used in Masonic ceremonies, e.g. "cowans" and "tyler," appear derived from the French "couenne" (ignorant person) and "tailleur" (cutter), respectively. However, it should be noted that the origin of the word "cowan" is extremely difficult to trace. One of the characters in Masonic mythology—Hiram Abif—may also have a name derived from the French "Hiram a biffe" (Hiram who was eliminated or killed). Finally, the name Freemason may derive from the French "frère Mason" (brother Mason). These linguistic derivations may clarify some of the puzzling aspects of Masonic rites and may indicate an origin within the French Knights Templar. Are there any historical indications of a direct continuity between the Templars and the Freemasons?

The English Rebellion of 1381

The author John Robinson maintains that clues to the origin of the Freemasons can be found in a dramatic and tumultuous event in English history, the rebellion of 1381. There is no doubt that this violent episode could not have arisen without widespread grievances and dissatisfaction with the government of England; Robinson, however, proposes that the rebellious impulses of this movement were in part guided and taken advantage of by organized forces in sympathy with the Templars. How can this proposal be evaluated?

The circumstances in existence prior to the rebellion point to increasing miseries and tension that should have been anticipated by any sensible government. During the preceding three decades, outbreaks of bubonic plague (the Black Death) had caused tremendous mortality and depleted the population in the countryside. Affluent landowners could no longer totally depend upon the forced labor of their *villeins,* or serfs, to till the fields, and were forced to seek free laborers who worked for pay.

Normally, this labor shortage would have led to pay increases for free laborers, but this market mechanism was partly thwarted by a continually renewed piece of legislation called the Statute of

Laborers, which strove to keep wages fixed. While this statute was not universally enforced, it inspired tremendous resentment in the common people. On top of this, decades of less than effective war with France had incurred massive expenditures from the treasury. In spite of these expenditures, an alliance between the French and Spanish navies allowed joint raids by the French admiral Jean de Vienne and the Spaniard Ferran Sanches de Tovar upon Hastings and other English territories. So when a court official named John Legge started to administer a poll tax that further exacerbated the financial burden of the common people, resentment was at the boiling point (Oman, 1964, p. 27).

Violence first broke out in Essex at the end of May, 1381, when peasants refused to pay the poll tax and expelled the tax collector from their village. The next day, mounted messengers from both Essex and from London spread the word that the time of resistance was at hand. When judge Robert Belknap arrived from London to enforce tax collection, he was violently expelled and three of his clerks were killed (Oman, 1964, p. 33; Robinson, p. 19).

On the same day (June 2), a similar confrontation between John Legge and rebellious taxpayers took place in Kent, just to the south of Essex. Men from Essex crossed the Thames to coordinate actions with this new site of rebellion, and a Kentish mob formed, freed a prisoner at Rochester Castle, and then moved on to Maidstone, where a man called Wat (Walter) Tyler was suddenly proclaimed to be their leader (Oman, 1964, p. 34; Robinson, 1989, p. 20). One of Tyler's first acts was to free John

Ball, a priest imprisoned a Maidstone for his ferocious denouncements of the luxuries and alleged scandals involving the Pope and the English Archbishop, Simon Sudbury. Ball immediately began a letter-writing campaign to numerous other priests and sympathizers, urging further insurrection.

Who was Wat Tyler? Available records do not contain this name, so nothing certain is known of his antecedents. Some historians have suggested that he had been a soldier in war-torn France, and certainly, his skill in guiding the violent action that was to come does support this suggestion. Wat Tyler might not even be his real name. John Ball is known to have directed some of his letters to a "John Nameless" (Oman, 1964, p. 35). In view of the extreme riskiness of revolting against the English crown, it would be understandable if prominent figures in a rebellion would have preferred to be known by aliases, in case of defeat and the need to disappear back into the population. Is it possible, as Robinson suggests, that "Wat Tyler" was in fact "Walter the Tyler," who took his name from a position in a Templar-related secret society that preceded the Freemasons?

As the rebellion spread, mobs from both Kent and Essex converged to form a mass of at least 10,000 men. They marched into London and began a week of destruction of public records and property. Particular fury was directed toward properties owned by the Knights Hospitallers, who had received the property taken from the Templars. The mobs burned the property of Robert Hales, Treasurer of England and Prior of the Knights Hospitallers, who was vilified as the greatest traitor of England. They then burned the priory of St. John's Clerkenwell, the headquarters of the Knights Hospitallers. In contrast, when rioters entered the principal church of the Knights Templar in England, they merely removed and destroyed public records stored in it, but did no damage to the church itself. Additional structures destroyed were the Fleet and Newgate prisons (Oman, 1964, p. 40; Robinson, 1989, p. 23).

Richard II had recently come to the throne and in 1381 was a boy of only fourteen years of age. Nevertheless, he courageously decided to leave the fortified Tower of London to meet with the rebels and discuss their demands at an open field at Miles End, outside of the city. At that meeting he agreed to general pardons for all the rebels and to begin the abolition of serfdom.

While the King was occupied at this meeting, Ball, Tyler, a London citizen named Thomas Farringdon, and several hundred followers took the opportunity to occupy the Tower of London. The drawbridge of this impressive fortress was traitorously opened to the rebels by an alderman, Walter Sibley (Oman, 1964, p. 39). Once inside, the rebels seized Archbishop Simon Sudbury, Hospitaller Prior Robert Hales, John Legge, and some associates and beheaded them, to the roaring approval of a large mob. This was the signal for more violence, which took place throughout London and resulted in the murders of at least 160 men.

When news of this violence reached the King, the meeting with the rebels was broken off and the King retired to quarters within the city. The entire situation seemed to favor the continued success of the rebels. But disaster struck on June 15, when Tyler attended a second meeting with the King. At this meeting, a man from Kent accused Tyler of being a highwayman. Tyler, angered at this accusation, drew a blade upon his accuser. This caused Mayor William Walworth to threaten Tyler with arrest for drawing a weapon in the presence of the King. Tyler then turned his attention to Walworth and attempted to stab him, but was unsuccessful due to the coat of chain mail that Walworth wore under his clothing. Walworth and an associate responded to this attack by drawing their swords and inflicting fatal wounds on the neck and shoulders of Tyler, who managed to spur his horse in an attempt to flee before succumbing (Oman, 1964, p. 47; Robinson, 1989, p. 27).

This event proved calamitous for the rebellion. Many of the rebels had melted away after hearing the King's promises of clemency and abolition of serfdom. The revolt had lost the sympathy of many Londoners, who had become alarmed at the growing loss of property and life. The King was able to rally loyalists and armed men to his cause, and the revolt was rapidly suppressed. The promises made to the rebels under duress by the King were withdrawn, and the status quo ante was gradually restored.

Legitimate questions about the Rebellion, however, remain. Uprisings had occurred in a variety of locations—Kent, Essex, and East Anglia—almost simultaneously. Was this evidence of an organized, coordinated action? Many students of history, including Winston Churchill, have long speculated that an organized society was partly responsible for the rebellion (Churchill, 1958, p. 372).

A royal letter written in July of 1381 complained about secret gatherings or secret confederacies in Cheshire (Robinson, 1989, p. 51). As noted above, numerous citizens of London helped initiate, coordinate, and sustain the rebellion, even though they had no direct connection with the tax collection incidents in Kent and Essex. The particular emphasis upon damaging the Knights Hospitallers, the enemies of the Templars, was striking. Rebels at York, numbering about 500, had all worn a common piece of clothing: a white, hooded shawl with a red decoration. These same colors had been worn by the Templars (Robinson, 1989, p. 58).

All of these clues suggest that an organized body of men with a definite, prearranged agenda had participated in the rebellion and had used it to further their own aims. Underground remnants of a Templar organization could well have been present during the rebellion. It is not at all unreasonable to propose that residual sympathy for the cause of the Templars had survived until 1381, since relatively few Templars were executed or imprisoned in England during their suppression, large numbers of resentful knights and associates must have remained within society. A rich, powerful military society like the Templars, which had existed for more than 200 years, cannot be made to completely disappear overnight.

A Painting by Hieronymus Bosch

Robinson has also uncovered another compelling indication that Freemasonry originated much earlier than is commonly thought

(Robinson, 1993). His argument is based on the surprising features of one painting by a famous artist, Hieronymus Bosch.

Bosch is one of the most well-known artists who worked in the fifteenth century. His family name was actually van Aken, but his name became associated with the small Dutch town of Hertogenbosch, in which he was born in 1450 (Gibson, 1973). Probably his most famous work is a painting entitled *The Garden of Earthly Delight,* which depicts a vivid assortment of demons and monsters devouring sinners in Hell. Bosch showed an intense passion for religious themes in his works and frequently railed against corruption in the Church by depicting debauched or thieving priests and nuns.

The curious painting examined by Robinson is entitled *The Wayfarer.* It shows a man walking down a country road with a staff in his hand and a pack on his back. He is walking away from a house with a decaying roof and associated with several disturbing characters: a woman and man lustfully embracing, and a man urinating into a field at the side of the house. The wayfarer is leaving this symbol of earthly folly and is approaching a pleasant field, surrounded by a fence guarded by a wooden gate. The boards on the gate are arranged in a very peculiar manner so as to form triangles that portray a Masonic symbol: a set square.

The pilgrim himself has notable peculiarities in dress. On one foot is a slipper instead of a shoe, and the pant leg above this foot is rolled up to the knee. This mode of dress is required during the initiation ceremony of a First Degree Mason; although these customs of initiation were established long ago, the exact reasons for them are not generally known. The wayfarer is carrying a hat in his hand, but is also wearing an apparently superfluous hood on his head, i.e., he is "hoodwinked" just like an applicant undergoing initiation into Freemasonry. Instead of being decorated by a customary feather, the wayfarer's hat is decorated by a plumb bob, a symbol of Masonic geometry. The wayfarer is carrying a pack upon his back that is supported by a rope around his neck, i.e., he is wearing a Masonic "cable tow." All of these peculiar features make a very convincing argument that Bosch was familiar with Masonic symbolism and that Freemasonry existed as early as 1480 (Robinson, 1993, p. 118). It also supports the general proposition that works of art can contain hidden Masonic messages, visible and comforting to the knowledgeable insiders who can discern them, but hidden to the enemies of Masonry.

The Priory of Sion

In his books, Lincoln and associates make a case for the existence of another secret society, long hidden, but somehow connected, to both the Templars and the Masons. The evidence presented for this derives from a collection of privately printed documents on file in the Bibliotheque Nationale of France in Paris. The most prominent of these documents is a manuscript called *Les Dossiers Secrets*, published in 1956. This document makes the claim that the Priory of Sion was a secret society founded to guide the Knights Templar. A list of twenty-six Grand Masters of the Priory is provided, beginning with a French knight named Jean de Gisors, who held the office in 1188, and ending with Jean Cocteau, the well-known French artist who allegedly held the office up until his death in 1963 (Baigent, 1996, p. 133).

One surprising feature of this list of Grand Masters is that it includes such illustrious names as Leonardo da Vinci, Botticelli, Robert Boyle, and Isaac Newton! If this list is valid, it indicates that some of the most influential people in European history were all involved with the goals of a hidden, secret society! By an analysis of the biographies of all of these supposed Grand Masters, Lincoln was able to show that many of them were surprisingly interconnected through the years via acquaintances, patrons, and loyalties. Also, even Newton and da Vinci had surprisingly intense interests in unorthodox religious ideas and esoteric philosophies. Newton, for instance, was convinced that the dimensions of the pyramids held some kind of clue to ancient wisdom about the nature of the universe, and spent years trying to analyze and decode them (Tompkins, 1971, pp. 30–31). In 1703 Newton became a close associate of Jean Desaguliers, who later in life became Grand Master of the Masonic Lodge in The Hague and was very active in extending the influence of Freemasonry in Europe (Baigent, 1996, p. 456). So the claim by Lincoln and Baigent that these illustrious artists and scholars might have participated in an esoteric, secret society is more plausible than one might think at first.

It is undeniable that a society called the Priory of Sion does exist today. Lincoln has even met with representatives of this society. However, it is less clear that this modern-day society has in fact continuously existed and striven for centuries to influence European events. Lincoln and co-authors have uncovered a reference to the Priory of Sion in a document dating from 1616 (Baigent, 1996, p. 171), and there is some evidence that its members might have belonged to another organization, the Compagnie de Saint-Sacrement. This society actively opposed some of the policies of Louis XIV and applied pressure for clemency for Nicholas Fouquet, the Finance Minister imprisoned at this time (see Chapter 4). Also, an old gravestone in the churchyard at Rennes-le-Chateau bears a carved inscription that does appear to make a cryptic reference to the Priory of Sion (Baigent, 1996, plate after p. 122).

Lincoln and Baigent have made extensive efforts to characterize the Priory of Sion. They have presented evidence that the parchments allegedly discovered by Sauniere that refer to the Priory of Sion were once in the possession (as stated by a notarized document) of one Roundell Cecil Palmer, Earl of Selbourne (Baigent, 1991, p. 248). The Earl of Selbourne was an eminent personality and during World War II served as the Minister of Economic Warfare, supervising intelligence operations behind German lines in Europe. He worked closely with Winston Churchill and the head of British Intelligence. This documented association of this respected and powerful personality with the Saunier parchments lends them some credibility. This information may also shine some light upon the use of the phrase "et in arcadia ego" by the novelist Evelyn Waugh, since Waugh traveled in the same circles as the Earl of Selbourne, was a close friend of Randolph Churchill, and might have had access to information about the documents and about the Sauniere manuscripts.

The proposition that the Sauniere parchments might have been of some interest to these high-ranking members of British Intelligence is not quite as fanciful as it might appear. John le Carré, the English author of spy thrillers such as *The Spy Who Came in from the Cold,* recalled that during his service in the MI5 intelligence agency, a surprisingly large proportion of his co-workers were Freemasons (le Carré, 1993).

Other critics, however, have claimed that the modern-day Priory of Sion is nothing more than an informal philosophical organization in France that cloaks itself in mystery but in fact has no genuine antecedents in medieval Europe. The claim that the Priory of Sion has continuously existed as a society of secretive and powerful individuals is at this point still controversial and can only be regarded as unproven. If it does prove true, this would tend to explain the puzzling reference to "Sion" in the encrypted messages discovered by Abbe Sauniere.

What have we learned from these chapters? First, a natural pentagon of mountains, ideally located for sighting the positions of the sun and moon, exists at Rennes-le-Chateau. This penta-gon is located precisely at the only latitude where the sun-moon angles equal 72 degrees, an angle needed to construct pentago-nal and star-shaped figures. This is analogous to the natural rock formation at the Externsteine and the standing stones at Stone-henge, used for sighting the moon and sun at a latitude where the sun-moon angle equals 90 degrees, needed to construct another polygon, a rectangle.

Also, a collection of Templar structures was built upon the mountaintops at Rennes-le-Chateau, suggesting a continuing memory of the function of these pre-Christian sites within the Knights Templar. A similar situation applies to the cathedral at Aachen. Both sites may have been revered by pre-Christian societies, and may have served as rallying points by communities opposed to the central authority of the Catholic Church, e.g. the Saxons at Aachen and the Cathars at Rennes-le-Chateau. It seems possible that some efforts within the Knights Templar might have been directed at finding points of commonality between pre-Christian and Christian philosophies, which would have automatically created a conflict between the Templars and the central authority of the Church. There is some evidence that the Templars possessed information and relics that might have exacerbated this conflict.

The sites we have discussed so far are not the only ones that can be detected in Europe. Similar themes connected with pen-tagons and stars seem to be repeated in northern Spain.

＊

CHAPTER 7

Santiago de Compostela

S ANTIAGO DE COMPOSTELA, A SMALL TOWN LOCATED IN THE region of northwestern Spain called Galicia, is the site of one of the oldest and most revered religious shrines in Christendom (Fig. 14). It has been famous throughout Europe for 1,200 years as the burial site of St. James, the brother of John, the son of Zebedee, a disciple of Jesus (Acts 12:2). This site has a long history, partly obscured by mysteries and myth.

The history traditionally ascribed to Santiago can be briefly summarized. St. James is alleged to have traveled to Spain to spread the Gospel for six years, then returned to the Holy Land, where he was beheaded by Herod. His remains were then carried by boat to Spain and then transferred across the Iberian peninsula to their resting place in Galicia. His tomb was revered for several centuries, but during the time of Roman persecution of Christians under the Emperor Diocletian, the local Christian community became dispersed and the location of the tomb was forgotten.

This area of Spain retained the identity of an independent kingdom for many years until finally coming under the rule of the Visigoths in A.D. 585. The influence of the Visigoths was then overturned by the arrival of the Muslim Moors in Spain in A.D. 711; however, Moorish influence in Galicia was very limited, so that an independent Christian kingdom in nearby Asturias was allowed to exist. Then, in A.D. 813, a local religious hermit reported seeing a bright star shining down upon an oak tree on top of a hill and hearing celestial music. These events prompted an investigation of the site and the re-discovery of St. James's tomb, marked with an inscription. Shortly afterwards, King Alfonso II of Asturias established a church on the spot, which soon began to attract pilgrims from all over Europe.

The name of the town which grew up around the tomb, Santiago de Compostela, seems to have been derived from several words: *Sant Iago* (Spanish for "Saint James") and *campus stellae* (Latin for "field of the star") (Crow, 1985, p. 83; Stokstad, 1978, p. 6).

As the fame and importance of Santiago increased, the original, humble church built there was torn down and replaced with a much larger one in A.D. 900. Pilgrimages to Santiago were first organized by monks of the French congregation of Cluny (Stokstad, 1978, p. 10). The second church at Santiago in turn was destroyed by the Moorish general Almanzor, who confiscated its doors and church bells for incorporation into the great mosque

Fig. 14

Map of Spain

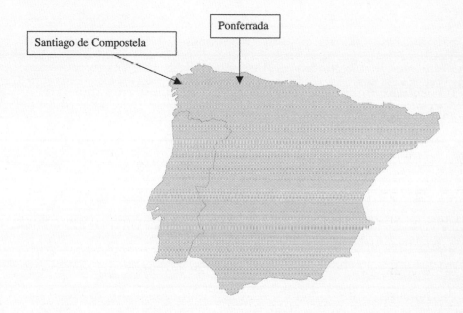

located to the south at Cordoba. A third church was constructed beginning in 1027, but was itself torn down and replaced by a new cathedral, dedicated by Pope Urban II in A.D. 1105. Thenceforth, Santiago was put under the supervision of a Benedictine order of French monks, who also supervised the pilgrimage routes leading through southern France. In 1164, the military and religious order of St. James of the Sword was founded, much like the Knights Templar, to protect the pilgrimage road leading to Santiago. Over the years, thousands of pilgrims traveled to Santiago from all over Europe, and an extensive collection of religious and other buildings accumulated around the cathedral (Stokstad, 1978, p. 10).

It is noteworthy that the location of Santiago, supposedly inspired by a vision of a star, matches the latitude of Rennes-le-Chateau precisely: Both are located at 42.7 degrees north of the equator. Also, like the region of Rennes-le-Chateau, there is an abundance of megalithic monuments in the area: Twelve dolmens and burial sites are found near Santiago, the most prominent being a structure called the Dolmen of Tordoya, located about eighteen miles north of Santiago. Megalithic structures are in general very numerous in northern Spain, and various methods of dating suggest that they are older than the structures at Stonehenge. Some archeologists believe that the entire tradition of megalithic architecture might have originated in northern Spain (Service, 1979, p. 80). Is there any connection between these pre-Christian structures and the building of the Christian religious monuments in Santiago?

Before we can approach this question, a more careful look at the history of Santiago is in order.

Who Is Buried at Santiago de Compostela?

The belief that St. James is buried at Santiago de Compostela has not been questioned for centuries in Spain. How plausible is this tradition?

A twentieth century archeological excavation has confirmed the great age of the tomb, which has now been incorporated into the cathedral at Santiago. Originally, the tomb was located in a Roman cemetery besides the principal north-south road of Galicia, constructed perhaps as early as A.D. 100. Behind the tomb is a massive Roman wall later used by builders as part of the cathedral. There was an extensive Roman presence in Galicia; in fact, the world's only Roman lighthouse, still in good working condition, stands at La Coruña, some forty miles north of Santiago. So there is good evidence for the antiquity of the tomb, and complementary evidence that the area possessed a port that connected it to the trade routes within the Roman Empire.

It is not impossible that travel between the Holy Land and Galicia could have taken place in ancient times. In support of this, some scholars believe that King Herod Antipas actually was exiled to Gaul in southern France after the debacle of his rule in Israel (Andrews, 1996, p. 10). Also, a verse in the New Testament (Romans 15:24–28) discusses St. Paul's intentions to travel to Spain. But these facts do not unequivocally identify the skeletal remains that are buried in Santiago as belonging to St. James. In fact, there are other possible candidates for the inhabitant of this tomb.

Some scholars believe that the person interred at Santiago was not St. James, but a local cleric, Priscillian of Avila, whose unorthodox views of religion brought him into conflict with the Church. Priscillian's heretical views included a denial of the existence of the Trinity and use of a non-canonical book, the Acts of Thomas (we'll discuss this book later). Priscillian observed the Sabbath on Saturday, after the Jewish practice (and indeed, as Jesus must have observed it). One of Priscillian's followers, a woman named Eregia, travelled to the Holy Land and to Edessa in Turkey in A.D. 381 to seek additional non-canonical scripts, that is, old religious writings that had not been admitted into the Bible by the Catholic Church (Baigent, et al., 1986, p. 113). All these practices led to the execution of Priscillian for heresy in A.D. 385; afterwards, his remains were brought back to his native Galicia in Spain. It is possible that the tomb of this local holy man somehow became identified as the tomb of St. James (Fletcher, 1984, p. 59).

Another possible candidate for the person buried at Santiago is not St. James, the disciple of Jesus, but James the Just, the brother of Jesus.

James, the brother of Jesus? When I first came upon a reference to this James, I was incredulous. If such a person did exist, why had I never heard of him before? In fact, however, my skeptical attitude seems to have been in error, since considerable evidence for the existence of James the Just exists, and has been summarized in a fascinating book by Robert Eisenman, professor of Middle Eastern religions at California State University (Eisenman, 1997). There are sparse references to brothers and sisters of Jesus in the New Testament; one reference (Gal. 1:18-20) (Eisenman, 1997, p. 74) notes that Paul met with St. Peter and with James, the brother of the Lord. James and Peter apparently disagreed over the issue of whether Jews should break bread with Gentiles (Gal. 2:11-12; see also Mark 6:3).

There are also old, extra-Biblical references to James. Some of these are in the writings of Hegesippus, a cleric from Palestine who lived between A.D. 90-180. His original writings have not survived, but are quoted in the *Ecclesiastical History* by Eusebius of

Caesarea, another Church historian who lived between A.D. 260 and 340. These references state that James the Just, the brother of Jesus, was elected an early bishop of the original Church in Jerusalem after Jesus' crucifixion. James retained this position of authority until his execution by the Romans in A.D. 62. The burial marker of James has been located in the Kedron valley near Jerusalem (Eisenman, 1997, p. 621) (Schonfield, 1974, p. 217).

Recently, the discovery of a stone artifact in Jerusalem has stimulated a renewed interest in James the Just. This item is a twenty-inch-long limestone box called an ossuary that in ancient times was used to store the bones of the deceased. This box is inscribed with the following words using the Hebrew characters of ancient Aramaic: "Ya'akov bar Yosef a khui Yeshua." These words translate to "Jacob (James in English) the son of Joseph and brother of Joshua (Jesus)." The box's owner, a collector, showed it to Andre Lemaire, a French scholar. He recognized the archaic form of some of the Aramaic letters as the language commonly spoken in ancient Israel and corresponding to a cursive form of writing used between A.D. 10 and 70 in the famous Dead Sea Scrolls (Lemaire, 2002). These ancient scrolls contain portions of the Old Testament together with the records of a Jewish religious sect, the Essenes, which existed in Israel until the first century B.C. Judging from the inscription, this box does appear to date from around the time of Jesus.

If genuine, this box might at one time have held the remains of James the Just. It also represents the earliest archeological reference to Jesus. Previously, the earliest reliable reference to Jesus was present on a papyrus fragment of the Gospel of John dating to A.D. 125 (Gugliotti, 2002). The inscription on the box, of course, could have been forged at some later time to deceive a buyer, but the amount of wear on the inscription appears to match the surface properties of the rest of the box. Another point is that the inscription might refer to some other persons named James and Jesus rather than the subjects of the New Testament. Lemaire, however, calculates that for a contemporary population of about 80,000, the chances of even these relatively common three names being linked together by chance is relatively low. So it is possible that the box may represent one of the most precious relics from the time of the New Testament if it does not prove fraudulent.

If the box ever contained the bones of James, it is empty now. The location of James' actual remains are not known. The possibility that they were transferred to Spain at some point in time seems no less improbable or probable than the chance that the remains of the other James, St. James the Great, are in Spain. The locations of the graves and remains of all the New Testament figures is also problematic. St. Peter's Basilica in Rome, for example, has been revered as the resting place of St. Peter since the second century A.D. There are indeed catacombs beneath the basilica that do contain human remains, but it is not possible archeologically to state with complete certainty that they are in fact the bones of St. Peter.

Some scanty information about other relatives of Jesus, in addition to James the Just, is also available. For example, Eusebius reports that the Roman Emperor Domitian questioned descendents of Jesus' relatives about their ancestry in the first century A.D. In A.D. 318, eight later descendents of Jesus' relatives met with Pope Sylvester to demand the re-establishment of their authority over churches in Jerusalem. Since the Church of Rome was then beginning to occupy the central position of authority in Christendom, this request was denied (Baigent, 1997, p. 472).

The real meaning of the tomb at Santiago de Compostela depends upon the identity of the person buried there. An unorthodox or heretical tradition may underlie the tomb if either James the Just or Priscillian were buried there. Like similar challenges to religious orthodoxy by the Cathars at Rennes-le-Chateau or the Saxons at the Externsteine, these traditions could later have been concealed by later constructions and decrees by the Orthodox Church. On the other hand, there may be no real connection between the Holy Land and Santiago de Compostela, in spite of centuries of religious tradition asserting such a connection. This riddle may not be resolvable by archeological methods or through the sparse historical documentation that has survived.

Thus far, we have established only a few common themes between Rennes-le-Chateau and Santiago de Compostela. Both sites possess megalithic structures; both sites may involve unorthodox religious thinking that came into conflict with the Church; and the "star" theme in the name of Santiago de Compostela seems to recapitulate the pentagonal and star themes present in the geographical positions of structures around Rennes-le-Chateau. Both sites show some connections with the Templars:

For example, there is a major Templar church at Mosteiro, a few miles south of Santiago de Compostela (Atienza, 1985, p. 16). Both sites are located at the precise latitude (42 degrees, 50 minutes N) required for the sun–moon angle to equal the pentagonal angle of 72 degrees. Are any astronomical alignments detectable at the site of Santiago de Compostela?

A modern-day street map of Santiago, such as those available in tourist guides or map stores, shows a profusion of churches and other buildings that have been built over the centuries near the cathedral. No obvious star-shaped or pentagonal arrangement of buildings is discernable around the cathedral. One map published in a book by Stokstad (Stokstad, 1978, p. 2) does, however, hint that some astronomical alignments may be detectable at Santiago. During the eleventh century, a series of fortified walls were constructed around the cathedral. At intervals, the walls were interrupted by gates that led to roads, particularly for the pilgrimage road that led to France. One of the gates, near the current location of the Plaza de San Roque, is positioned at 51 degrees from true north, relative to the cathedral. Another gate, located near the current-day position of the Church of St. Felix, is positioned at 132 degrees from true north, relative to the cathedral. These positions correspond to lines pointing to the maximal standstill points of the full moon at the winter solstice and summer solstice, respectively (Fig. 15). See Tables 1 and 2 for the lunar positions at the latitude of Rennes-le-Chateau.

These astronomical alignments may be purely coincidental, or, on the other hand, may reflect connections between ancient

Fig. 15

Possible Astrological Alignments at Santiago

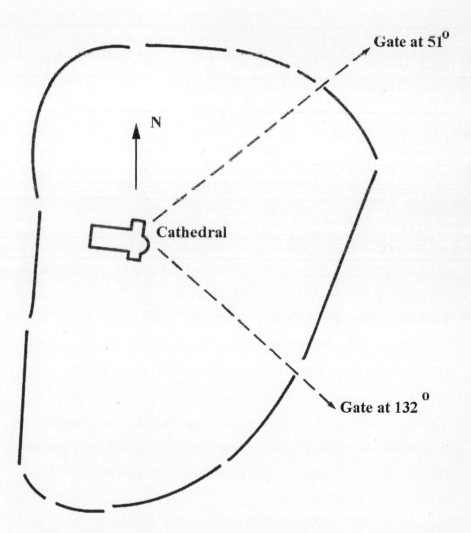

structures that have been covered by the more modern structures of the cathedral and medieval gates. Only an on-site inspection of these locales could provide more information. But it is not likely that traces of megalithic structures could have survived the continual process of construction in the area. So, aside from the "star" theme in the name of Santiago de Compostela, there is no conclusive evidence for astronomy at this site. However, other closely related sites in Spain do show an interest in astronomy.

Astronomy and Other Sites in Spain

The area to the east of Santiago de Compostela has been well described in a charming book by Jack Hitt, *Off the Road: A Modern-day Walk Down the Pilgrim's Route into Spain.* Hitt is an American who decided to replicate the medieval experiences of pilgrims to Santiago by walking across northern Spain from France. Several of his observations are of interest to us (Hitt, 1989, p. 11).

Hitt followed the original pilgrimage road built to carry pilgrims from the rest of Europe across northern Spain. The route was actually composed of four different roads, leading from Paris, Vezelay, Le Puy, and from Arles (passing through Carcassone, just north of Rennes-le-Chateau) that converged into one road near Pamplona, Spain. Two sites located along the road show connections to astronomy.

The first site is the church located at San Juan de Ortega, near the town of Burgos. This well preserved church is over a thousand years old. It was constructed to face due east and west, so that precisely at 5 P.M. on the day of the Equinox in March, a beam of light passes through a window to illuminate a representation of the Annunciation. In bygone times, pilgrims would deliberately time their passage along the pilgrimage road to observe this phenomenon (Hitt, 1989, p. 98). This church was constructed with the same attention to astronomy that is evident in the cathedral at Chartres, which preserved a pre-Christian focus upon the sun and the moon, and in the cathedral at Aachen.

The other site of interest is the castle at Ponferrada, located considerably closer to Santiago. This is the largest Templar castle in northern Spain. The wall surrounding the castle grounds was built in the shape of an irregular pentagon, and surmounted by twelve towers, which scholars have determined represent the constellations of the Zodiac (Hitt, 1989, p. 166; Luengo, 1980, p. 131). Some Spanish authors have maintained that the names of the constellations corresponding to these towers, which are not in the same order as the constellations in the Zodiac, spell out some sort of secret code related to Templar practices. Inspection of the stones composing the castle reveals that many are decorated by inscribed marks, called mason's marks, that identified the craftsmen who shaped them. One of these mason's marks is a tilted star that precisely matches the tilted, star-shaped figure that was hidden in the manuscript found by Abbe Sauniere at Rennes-le-Chateau (Luengo, 1980, p. 135). Thus, it is clear that the same sort of preoccupations with astronomy, stars, and pentagons that we have seen at Rennes-le-Chateau also apply to these ancient structures on the pilgrimage road leading to San- tiago de Compostela.

There is a tradition that some sort of Templar secret is con- tained within the walls of the castle at Ponferrada. Some Spanish enthusiasts have petitioned the Spanish government, thus far in vain, for permission to excavate within the castle to seek some sort of Templar relic, perhaps the Holy Grail or even the Ark of the Covenant (see Neyman, 1998). Why would such fantastic notions have come to be associated with a Templar castle in Spain?

✳

CHAPTER 8

The Templars and the Holy Grail

T HE TEMPLARS HAVE LONG BEEN ASSOCIATED WITH A
religious relic called the Holy Grail. This relic is familiar
to us even today through such books as Thomas Malory's
fifteenth century *Morte d'Arthur*, or later works by Tennyson *(Idylls
of the King)* or T. H. White *(The Once and Future King)*. The Grail
has even appeared in recent movies like *Monty Python and the Holy
Grail* and *Indiana Jones and the Last Crusade*. But what was the Grail
and how did it come to be associated with the Templars?

This question is actually more difficult to answer than one
might think. The Holy Grail (or "Sangraal" in French) was the subject of at least eight different manuscripts written between 1190
and A.D. 1220. The most well known of these were Chretien de
Troye's *Le Comte del Graal*, Robert de Boron's *Joseph d'Arimathie*
and Wolfram von Eschenbach's *Parzifal*.

In the first tale, the Grail was described as a golden platter that served food. In other tales, the Grail was described as a carved or "fashioned" likeness of the head of Jesus that "could not have been made by human hands." In the story by Robert de Boron, the Grail was a cup that had been used at the Last Supper and which had collected the blood of Jesus during the Crucifixion. In *Parzifal*, the Grail was described as a magical stone, kept in a castle in the Pyrenees guarded by the Knights Templar (in the other tales, it was guarded by the Knights of King Arthur). Thus, the Grail is depicted in these stories as completely different things (Phillips, 1996, pp. 101–110).

The author of *Parzifal* claimed the tale originated from an ancient Arabic manuscript found in Toledo, Spain. Many of these tales, despite having been written in continental Europe, refer to events in England. A common theme is that the Grail was carried from the Holy Land by Joseph of Arimathea, who took responsibility for Jesus' burial, and somehow traveled with the Grail to England.

It is clear that these stories had a wide audience and influence in medieval Europe and continue to fascinate us today. But do they refer to any discernable historical reality? What exactly was the Grail? Henry Lincoln and co-authors have speculated that there is a meaning to the term that transcends a description of any physical object. They have proposed that the title is a play on words: "Sangraal" or "Sangreal" may actually refer to the combination of two French words—"Sang" and "Real," medieval French for "Holy Blood" (Baigent, et al., 1997, p. 320). In other words, the Holy Grail may have been a disguised reference to Holy Blood, the bloodline of Jesus that continued after him through the descendents of his family. This is only one of many speculations about the Holy Grail that is difficult to prove or disprove one way or another.

A recent student of the subject, Dr. Graham Phillips, has focused his attention on a later manuscript dating from A.D. 1330 titled *La Folie Perceval*. Because of its later date, many scholars have dismissed this story as merely having been derived from the earlier ones. However, some textual details suggest that this story is a copy of one that actually preceded the other Grail stories (Phillips, 1996, p. 153). Curiously, the adventures of its English hero, Percival, correspond closely in many respects with the life history of an actual historical figure named Payne Peveril who lived in A.D. 1070 and whose name is similar to the fabled Percival.

Peveril was descended from a sixth century Welsh warrior named Owain Ddantgwyn. At the time when Owain Ddantgwyn lived, many Celtic warriors adopted the name of an animal, such as a dog or a dragon, as a battle name. King Arthur's father, Uther Pendragon, for example, supposedly appended the title of dragon to his name. The real Owain Ddantgwyn is known to have been called the Bear warrior. The Welsh word for bear is *arth,* whereas the Latin for bear is *ursus*. A combination of the two words could have created the new name of Arthur, associated with Owain Ddantgwyn. Phillips makes a very convincing case that this person was indeed the historical King Arthur.

The very existence of a historical King Arthur has been hotly debated and considered by some to be mythical. One of the earliest documents that offers a relatively complete account of Arthur was written by a Welsh cleric, Geoffrey of Monmouth, in about A.D. 1135. Some of the details of Geoffrey's account, such as the names of Arthur's relatives, seem consistent with other historical records, whereas other "facts" and dates in this document are clearly inaccurate or fabricated. However, at least two other documents from about the same period also mention Arthur, so some historical figure of that name, a local chieftain, if not a king, seems likely to have existed (Phillips, 1996, p. 8). The existence of a historical Arthur has recently been supported by the finding of a stone bearing a sixth century Latin version of the name Arthur at the Welsh castle of Tintagel (San Jose Mercury News, August 7, 1998).

The basic proposal of Phillips's book was that an unorthodox religious community was present in the region of Wales ruled by Arthur (Owain Ddantgwyn). Relics associated with this community were thus guarded by Arthur, and perhaps passed down to his descendents. Stories about the adventures of one descendent, Payne Peveril, became transformed into the Grail stories within a century after his death, and thus connected the Holy Grail with tales of Percival and King Arthur.

This explanation still does not specify what the Grail was, or indeed, if the various types of Grails identified in the stories corresponded to physical artifacts. Also, all the Grail tales have elements of unorthodox religious principles in them, for example, that the apostolic succession and the secrets of the Mass did not pass down from Jesus to Peter, but from Jesus to Joseph of Arimathea and the subsequent guardians of the Grail. This peculiar religious context of the Grail, as well as the identity of the Grail, may relate directly to the Knights Templar. Which of the many different objects identified as the Grail was linked to the historical King Arthur, and which one can be associated with the Templars?

The Grail story studied by Phillips, *La Folie Perceval,* introduces yet another variant of the Grail. In this story, the Grail is a holy book that contains the secret words of Jesus (Phillips, 1996, p. 153). Such a book, in fact, is actually known to exist. The complete text of this book, called the Gospel of Thomas, was only discovered in 1945, when Egyptian peasants digging near the village of Nag Hammadi found ceramic jars containing leatherbound manuscripts written in Coptic, and dating from A.D. 400. One manuscript was a collection of sayings of Jesus, some of which were already known from the other canonical Gospels, and some of which were new. Seven verses of this unorthodox Gospel of Thomas precisely matched verses in another fragment of manuscript discovered elsewhere in 1895 and which could be dated to at least as early as A.D. 150 (Baigent, 1997, p. 402; Phillips, 1996, p. 166).

This manuscript represents an early Christian document that in later centuries was excluded from the orthodox New Testament by the Church. It is possible that Christian communities on the fringes of Rome's influence, such as in Wales or Spain, could have retained this and other non-orthodox works and secretly concealed them for many years. The Gospel of Thomas is one logical explanation for the description of the Holy Grail that was connected with Arthur.

Are there other types of Grails present in other stories that have been linked with the Knights Templar? Phillips has suggested a number of other artifacts, such as medieval cups and carved like-nesses of Jesus, that could explain these other variants of the Grail. However, an even more interesting possibility has recently been raised: a link between the Holy Grail, the Knights Templar, and the Shroud of Turin.

The Knights Templar and the Shroud of Turin

The Shroud of Turin is a religious artifact that has attracted immense publicity and controversy over the last twenty years. Its general features are well known. It consists of a long linen cloth with two regions of a faint brown discoloration that clearly show images of the front and back of the body and face of a crucified, bearded man. The first indisputable record of the Shroud consists of a religious medallion that had been dropped into the Seine which bears a clear image of the Shroud. This medallion can be dated to A.D. 1338. Thus, the Shroud dates at least from medieval times and is clearly very old. What is now being debated intensely is whether or not the Shroud is the genuine burial shroud of Jesus.

Debate over this question focuses on at least two issues: 1) is the Shroud really old enough to date from the time of the Crucifixion, and 2) is the image on the Shroud genuine or merely the work of an extremely able medieval forger? These questions are difficult to answer, and have been discussed in great detail in a recent book by a long-term investigator of the Shroud, Ian Wilson (Wilson, 1998).

The question of whether or not the image on the Shroud is a simple forgery seems most amenable to resolution. The image on the Shroud is a faint brown discoloration, showing no outlines or brushstrokes, and colors only the most superficial layer of the linen fibers. It clearly is not painted. A number of investigators have attempted to duplicate the image by draping heated metal statues and creating scorch marks on cloths, but their results have not generally been convincing. The image itself shows anatomically correct patterns of blood flow from wounds in the feet and wrists and displays numerous tiny scourge marks on the back and apparent bruises on the knees. The regions of the Shroud corresponding to the soles of the feet of the crucified man show minute particles of dirt. It seems almost inconceivable that a medieval forger could have created such a convincing forgery.

In fact, it is not necessary to invoke some sort of forgery to explain the image; nor is a supernatural explanation necessarily needed. As Wilson has noted, there exist other examples where contact between cloth and dying or dead tissues has resulted in a discoloration on cloth that mimics the appearance of the tissue. For example, in 1981 in Liverpool, a patient dying in a hospital of pancreatic cancer left a surprising discoloration on his sheets that showed remarkably clear impressions of his hands and legs (Wilson, 1998, p. 209). The phenomenon may be related to pigmented molecules generated during pathophysiological states.

Analysis of the chemical composition of the image on the Shroud has suggested the presence of trace amounts of bilirubin, a molecule that can produce highly colored, brownish-yellow stains. When red blood cells are ruptured, their released hemoglobin is broken down into molecules of bilirubin. Normally, bilirubin is in turn degraded in the liver and does not reach high concentrations in the bloodstream. However, in some newborns, the liver has not yet matured enough to perform this function, resulting in high blood levels of bilirubin and the skin discoloration known as neonatal jaundice. Fortunately, this is easily treated, since bilirubin is a light-sensitive pigment and can be destroyed by exposing the skin of a newborn to radiation from ultraviolet lights (Guyton, 1971, p. 864; McDonagh, 2001; Raethel, 1975). Exposure of bilirubin to ultraviolet light converts the bilirubin into molecular forms that are more water soluble and more easily removed from the blood by the body.

Conceivably, the extreme stress caused by crucifixion could have an analogous damaging influence upon the liver, resulting in elevated levels of bilirubin beneath the skin that could have been transferred to a burial shroud. Similarly, pancreatic tumors can in some cases encroach upon the common bile duct, impairing the transport of bilirubin from the liver into the gall bladder or into the duct that drains bilirubin into the intestine for excretion. As a result, bilirubin is unable to escape from the body and accumulates in the bloodstream (Sakurai, 2001). Thus, both crucifixion and pancreatic cancer might be expected to increase levels of bilirubin in the blood and cause some traces of it to be transferred to cloth covering the skin.

If cloth saturated with bilirubin is both in contact with human skin and also exposed to bright sunlight, some interaction between light and bilirubin in a burial shroud could perhaps have resulted in the "photographic" qualities of the image on the Shroud. Skin absorbs almost 40 percent of the energy of short, ultraviolet wavelengths of light, but reflects 96 percent of the energy in long wavelengths of light (Anderson, 1981; Vogel, 1991). Thus, light passing through a cloth and reflecting off of skin back up through the cloth should be depleted in ultraviolet wavelengths. Bilirubin in a cloth should be less altered by reflected UV light when the cloth is covering skin than when the cloth is placed over empty spaces. One could propose that cloth near skin should retain more unaltered bilirubin, which is less water soluble and more difficult to remove from cloth by washing, than cloth far away from skin. Bilirubin thus could be part of a plausible explanation of how a brownish-yellow stain could interact with light to form a faint image on cloth.

Even if this rather fanciful explanation proves difficult to confirm by experimentation, our incomplete understanding of how the image on the Shroud was formed is not sufficient grounds to dismiss it out of hand as an artificial forgery.

The other question, that of the age of the Shroud, is a far more serious one. As noted above, the earliest secure historical record of the Shroud dates from A.D. 1338. What other information can be used to estimate the age of the Shroud?

Other artistic representations of Jesus and his burial seem to clearly represent the image on the Shroud, even though these representations do not name the Shroud explicitly. For example, a picture in the so-called "Hungarian Pray" manuscript, dating from A.D. 1192, shows a burial shroud of Christ that contains a distinctive pattern of small holes that precisely matches a pattern of holes that puncture a region of the Shroud (Wilson, 1998, p. 141). Also, distinctive features of the image of the face on the Shroud match details of several representations of Christ that date from very early times. These features on the Shroud include small marks on the forehead and cheek regions that are caused by irregularities in the weave of the cloth. Many of these extraneous irregularities appear in early painted depictions of Christ, e.g. in the Panziano catacombs of Rome, dating from A.D. 700, and in the Church of Daphni near Athens, dating from A.D. 1100. (Wilson, 1998, p. 141). Wilson has suggested that these early paintings were in fact copied from the image on the Shroud. Wilson and others have proposed that the Shroud was carried from the Holy Land and was hidden for centuries in the Turkish city of Edessa, until it was rediscovered and transferred to Constantinople in the seventh century. Subsequently, during the sack of Constantinople by the Crusaders in the thirteenth century, it came into the possession of Western knights and finally arrived in Europe, where its earliest confirmable historical record begins.

This proposed history of the Shroud does not in itself prove that it was derived from Jesus. It could possibly have originated from any one of the thousands of crucifixions that were the ultimate punishment throughout the cruel empire of Rome over hundreds of years. The features of the wounds depicted on the Shroud do, however, closely correspond to those described in the New Testament.

This very compelling historical and artistic evidence for the antiquity of the Shroud was contradicted recently by another type of evidence: Carbon-14 dating of small portions of the Shroud by several different laboratories indicated that it could not have been made any earlier than A.D. 1300. Thus, there is a distressing contradiction between historical-artistic and physical methods of dating the Shroud. Which method should be accepted?

The answer to this question depends upon how much faith an observer has in physical vs. historical-artistic methodology. Both methodologies are subject to errors in technique and interpretation. The historical-artistic approaches can be labeled as partly subjective. The radiocarbon method has had its own problems. Wilson notes that the accuracy of this method is not entirely unimpeachable: When a corpse of an ancient man was discovered buried in a peat bog in northern Europe (the so-called "Lindow man"), samples of tissue were distributed to several different labs to establish a date, using carbon-14 analysis. Each lab produced a different result: 300 B.C., A.D. 100, and A.D. 500! This disparity of results was rather unusual, and did not occur between labs studying the Shroud, but does point out that radiocarbon dating is not always infallible (Wilson, 1998, p. 192). Also, there is the possibility that contamination of the Shroud fibers by contact with generations of worshippers could have affected the dating results.

These objections do not just represent wishful thinking by adherents of the authenticity of the Shroud, but demonstrate the difficulty of generating absolutely accurate data about such a controversial artifact.

Regardless of whether or not the Shroud does date from the time of Christ, it is nevertheless clear that at some time in the twelfth or thirteenth centuries, it was regarded as the genuine, and perhaps miraculous, burial shroud of Christ by at least a considerable portion of worshippers. This belief may provide the connection between the Shroud, the Knights Templar, and the Holy Grail.

The Grail and the Shroud

There is some historical evidence pointing to a clear connection between the Holy Grail and the Shroud of Turin. The reason why this connection is not now generally appreciated stems from a incomplete knowledge of manuscripts describing the history of the Church.

The first of these errors in understanding appears to have been made in the eighth-century *History of the English Church* by Bede. In this book, and in the book upon which it was based (the *Liber Pontificales,* or "Book of the Popes," written in A.D. 530), the travels of St. Joseph of Arimathea and St. Phillip were described. In both books, the word "Britio" in Latin was mistakenly interpreted to mean "Britain." In fact, however, this word refers to a fortress in the Turkish city of Edessa (Britio Edessenarum). So, both books perpetuated the mistaken notion that Joseph of Arimathea traveled to Britain bearing the Grail. If he carried the Grail, it appears to have been carried to Edessa in Turkey. This is the site where the Shroud of Turin was initially hidden after allegedly leaving the Holy Land (Wilson, 1998, p. 169).

The second modern reappraisal of ancient manuscripts relevant to the Shroud involves a sixth century manuscript from the early Christian kingdom of Georgia, in the Caucasus south of Russia. This manuscript, first examined by a German scholar in 1901, states that St. Joseph of Arimathea collected Christ's blood in a headband and large sheet. This sheet conceivably could have been the Shroud of Turin, carried by Joseph of Arimathea to nearby Edessa.

How does this relate to the Templars? Records from the thirteenth century state that the Shroud was brought to Europe by a knight named Geoffrey de Charny. Somewhat later, in 1307, a knight named Geoffrey de Charny was one of two leading Templars to be burnt at the stake. If these two Geoffreys are one and the same man, as seems likely, it appears that the Shroud came into the possession of the Templars a few decades before their arrest and destruction on charges of heresy. It seems possible that the Templars regarded the Shroud as the true burial shroud of Christ, and revered it. A chance discovery made in Somerset, England, in the 1940s supports this contention. During repair of a wall of an old Templar preceptory, dating to A.D. 1280, an old wooden panel bearing an image of Christ strikingly similar to that of the Shroud was found. These findings suggest that the Shroud may have occupied a central place in the religious rites of the Templars.

All this information suggests that the Grail romances combined the descriptions of several religious relics into a variety of confused stories. One tradition in the stories may have described the retention of a non-canonical book by an unorthodox religious community in Britain that was safeguarded by a historical King Arthur and his descendents. Another root of the Grail romances may have originated in the acquisition of the Shroud of Turin by knights Templar during the Crusades. The modern question of whether or not the Shroud is a genuine artifact of the Crucifixion would not be relevant to medieval knights who did not question its sanctity.

Thus, the zeal of enthusiasts who search for the Holy Grail in the Templar Castle at Ponferrada in Spain may not be entirely misplaced, even if not strictly accurate. The Templars may very well have concealed the Grail, as well as other unorthodox religious and philosophical ideas, within their Order. Conceivably, the Templars may have sought reconciliation between unorthodox Christian thinking and the astronomy-based pre-Christian thought that was so prevalent in the regions the Templars controlled. Such a quest may have been a motivation for the placement of Templar monuments at the sites in Europe regarded as sacred by ancient astronomers and which dictated the construction of rectangles and pentagons.

CHAPTER 9

Astronomy and Religion
in Ancient Europe

THE SUBJECT DISCUSSED IN THE PRECEDING PAGES IS, actually, only a minor portion of data showing an influence of astronomy upon thinking and philosophies in ancient Europe. It has recently been demonstrated that sophisticated astronomical thinking played a major role in a religion that encompassed all of Europe and which was the major rival to Christianity. This religion was called Mithraism.

Mithraism, the Templars, and Freemasonry

Mithraism was a religious cult that dominated Europe between 100 B.C. and A.D. 300. Its adherents participated in a religious secret society that left no written records and allowed a full disclosure of its secrets to only the most elevated in its hierarchy. The only remaining evidence of its existence are hundreds of shrines to the god Mithras, mostly located in underground cata-combs that still exist, perfectly preserved, throughout Europe. Most of these shrines to Mithras were concentrated in Rome, Eastern Europe, and along the Rhine, but fewer numbers can be found in almost any location in Europe, including Spain (Ulansey, 1989, p. 5). As Christianity replaced Mithraism, churches were commonly built over the sites of Mithraic shrines; one of these was the original St. Peter's Basilica in Rome (Fideler, 1989, p. 145).

Within each shrine, typical Mithraic statues and mosaics por-trayed a puzzling array of men and creatures. It is only recently that the meaning of these statues, and their relationship to a wor-ship of an astronomical event, has been unraveled by David Ulansey, assistant professor of religion at Boston University. The main features of Mithraic statues and other symbolic objects were a depiction of the man-God Mithras, seated on the back of a bull and wearing a cape and pointed hat. While sitting on the bull, Mithras is shown to be plunging a knife into its neck, killing it. Frequently, this depiction was accompanied by smaller figures of a scorpion, a dog, a raven, a cup, and a lion (Fig. 16).

Some features of Mithraism seem strikingly reminiscent of the attitudes and symbolism found in Freemasonry. Each Mithraic painting or sculpture of the bull-slaying scene also contained pre-sentations of the sun and moon and planets represented as seven stars. As we have seen, Masonic Tracing Boards also contain these symbols. A common Mithraic symbol was a ladder with seven "gates" or spaces between the rungs that each represented one of

Fig. 16

Man-God Mithras

the seven levels attained by initiates progressing toward the utmost secret of the cult. The seven levels of Mithraism corresponded to the seven planets: Crow (Mercury), Bridegroom (Venus), Soldier (Mars), Lion (Jupiter), Perses (Moon), Sun-conveyer (Sun), and Father (Saturn) (Campbell, 1968, p. 288; Gordon, 1996, p. 143; Ulansey, 1989, p. 19). During initiation rites, participants would wear masks portraying crows or lions and would make cawing or roaring sounds (Meyer, 1987, p. 199). Masonic Tracing Boards also depict a ladder or staircase with three rungs that correspond to the three degrees of initiation (see McNulty, 1991, and Chapter 5).

Mithraic cults apparently never wrote down any of the secrets of the cult, but used an array of pictures and symbols that were coded for the secrets and were used as memory devices to instruct initiates. Since many Mithraic initiates in ancient times were probably unable to read, these symbolic devices only seem practical. Masonic Tracing Boards likewise only portray symbols without written explanations for them.

During one of the stages of the initiation rites of Mithraism, an initiate takes the place of the bull and is ceremonially "killed" by a participant so he can be reborn into a new life (Campbell, 1968, p. 297). An emperor of the late Roman Empire, Commodus, outraged his fellow Mithraic worshippers when he participated in such a ceremony by committing a genuine murder instead of a merely symbolic one (Campbell, 1968, p. 297). In the Third Degree ceremony of Freemasonry, an initiate is also ceremonially "killed" to commemorate the fate of Hiram Abif.

These similarities between the rites of Mithraism and of Freemasonry seem too numerous to disregard as mere coincidence.

Similarities between Mithraism and the rites of Freemasonry have been noted for some time; a hypothesis that Masonry partly derived from Mithraism was advanced as long ago as 1865 by the Reverend C. W. King (Mackey, 1996, p. 190). At about the same time, in 1869, a German scholar named K. B. Stark proposed an astronomical explanation for Mithraism (Ulansey, 1989, p. 15). This entire line of thought was blocked, however, by contemporary scholars such as the Belgian Franz Cumont, who maintained that Mithraism originated solely from a Persian mystery religion. Cumont stated that this religion was wholly transplanted to Europe and thus unrelated either to astronomy or to indigenous European thought. This viewpoint, which is now considered erroneous, prevailed in the nineteenth century and obstructed progress in understanding Mithraism. So the possibility that Mithraism and Freemasonry share a common origin and themes related to astronomy has not yet been re-explored in the light of modern scholarship.

How could the founders of Freemasonry have acquired a knowledge of this obscure and long-vanished cult? It is possible that the founders of Freemasonry were scholars and students of ancient rites and were able to rediscover these little-known details of Mithraic symbolism in the 1600s and adopt them to their own purposes. It may be more plausible, however, to propose that some of the components of Freemasonry may have been directly passed down from people who had actually observed these rites during the Middle Ages. Performance of Mithraic ritual was proscribed in Europe during the fifth century by the Byzantine Emperor Theodosius, and Mithraism gradually waned in Europe, perhaps lasting to the sixth century (Mackey, 1996, p. 191). However, Mithraism had flourished outside of Europe as well, as attested by Mithraic sites that have been found in Turkey at Pergamon and Tarsus, and in Palestine at Sidon and Sahin (Ulansey, 1989, p. 5). More tolerant attitudes towards Mithraism in the Middle East allowed it to persist for much longer than in Europe; Mithraic names and religious references still could be found in Iran as late as the twentieth century. Knights Templar who returned to Europe in the 1200s had been born and raised in the Holy Land. Many spoke some Arabic and were intimately familiar with religious and cultural practices of the Middle East. It is not unreasonable to suggest that returning Knights Templar may have adopted some aspects of Mithraic ritual for use in their own induction and initiation ceremonies and passed them down to the Masons.

What was the meaning of these puzzling practices and symbols, and why was Mithraism so popular in pre-Christian Europe? Ulansey and others have cracked the code that concealed the meaning of Mithraic symbols. The bull and other creatures in the symbolism have been revealed to signify constellations: Taurus, the Bull; Scorpio, the Scorpion; Canis major, the Dog, and so on. The killing of Taurus, the Bull, by the god Mithras represents an actual astronomical event: the precession of the equinoxes.

Before going into details about the astronomical discovery that inspired Mithraism, a brief review of concepts like the Zodiac and the equinox is in order.

The organization of a group of twelve stellar constellations into the Zodiac originates directly from ancient attempts to understand the movement of the sun in the sky throughout the year. If you were able to magically turn down the brilliance of the sun and dim its radiance so that stars would be visible even during the daytime, it would be possible to look up into the sky and see which stars appear to be directly "behind" the sun. For example, in the month of March, the sun occupies a position directly in front of the constellation of Pisces, the Fish. Naturally, this can't really be seen during the day, but if we wait for the vault of the heavens to "rotate" and drag the sun and stars towards the horizon, eventually the sun will appear to set and the stars associated with it will be visible.

The earth, however, is continually moving in its orbit around the sun. When we look at the sun in April, for example, the position of the earth in space has shifted, so that the line connecting the earth with the sun no longer points to Pisces, but has moved to point to Aquarius, the Water Carrier, which is directly behind the sun during that month. Thus, during the twelve months of the year, the sun will be located against twelve different backgrounds, or constellations, of stars, which include Scorpio, the Scorpion; Cancer, the Crab; Gemini, the Twins; Taurus, the Bull, and so forth. These twelve constellations, positioned in a line across the sky, form the Zodiac that is so celebrated by practitioners of astrology. The word Zodiac is similar to the word "zoo," since it derives from the Greek for "circle of animals" (Hawkins, 1983, p. 22).

The equinoxes are the times of the year when day length equals night length; one equinox occurs in the spring, and the other in the fall. Each year, the spring equinox occurs on the same day. On this day, in modern times, the sun sets in the constellation of Pisces. This occurs with great regularity, since the rotation of the earth and its orbit are very stable. However, this regularity and stability are not absolute, but change very slowly over thousands of years. This is because the north pole of the earth wobbles slightly, describing a small circle in space every 26,000 years. Hence, very slowly, the setting sun during the spring equinox changes its position relative to the constellations of the Zodiac. It appears to move from one constellation into another every 2,160 years. Several hundred years from now, the spring equinox will have moved into the constellation of Aquarius. Thus, the "dawning of the age of Aquarius" that was so happily proclaimed during the 1960s is actually several centuries away.

In some ways, this wobbling of the earth would seem to be surprising. The earth represents an extremely massive gyroscope, spinning in frictionless space. One would expect that its axis would be extremely stable. What causes the wobble?

The wobbling of the spinning earth happens because the earth is not a perfect sphere. The centrifugal force produced by the earth's spin causes a slight bulge to appear at the equator. Since the axis of the earth is tilted at an angle of 23.5 degrees away from the plane of its orbit around the sun, the gravitational fields of the sun and moon exert a force on these bulges to try to tug them back toward the plane of the ecliptic. This tug is not strong, but it is enough to cause this slow wobble of the axis.

Neither the precession of the equinoxes, nor the seasons themselves, would exist if the axis of the earth weren't tilted so strongly. This tilt is unusual in the solar system; most planets have an axis of rotation rather more perpendicular to their orbits. What caused this peculiar orientation of the earth?

The best explanation for this situation arises from study of many peculiar features of the earth and moon, along with geological data obtained from the moon rocks gathered by the Apollo missions. The earth-moon system is puzzling for several reasons. For one thing, the rates of rotation (angular momentum) of the earth and moon are considerably faster than would be expected. Also, the moon appears to lack an iron core, and seems to have an elemental composition that precisely matches the mantle of the earth. What accounts for these peculiar features of the earth and moon?

The most widely accepted explanation for these features is that the moon was created by a cataclysmic collision between the earth and a smaller, Mars-sized planet early in the life of the solar system 4.5 billion years ago. It appears that two planets once existed in the orbit of the present earth, and that the smaller planet overtook and collided with earth, knocking it off its axis and greatly increasing its rate of spin. An enormous cloud of debris, mainly derived from the mantle layers of the two planets, was kicked into space by the collision and gradually cooled down and coalesced into the moon. This would explain why the abundance of various isotopes of oxygen in moon rocks so closely matches the isotopic composition of rocks from the earth's mantle. The missing iron core of the moon was liquefied by the collision and being denser, sank into the interior of the earth. So the earth's axis of rotation and the wobble causing the precession of the equinoxes are both due to a catastrophic collision in the distant past (Spudis, 1996, p. 166).

This movement of the equinoxes is so slow and subtle that it was not detected by ancient sky-watchers for some time. Hipparchus apparently first recognized it in 125 B.C. He realized that the equinoctial sun had shifted its position into Aries (in Hipparchus' day) from the constellation of Taurus (Ulansey, 1989, p. 133). To us, this may seem like a mere astronomical curiosity. But to the ancients, who lacked our modern understanding of the nature of the solar system, this discovery must have had frightening implications. In those times, the earth was viewed as a stationary center surrounded by a cosmic sphere of stars. According to this viewpoint, in order to shift the equinoxes, some vast force must be causing the entire vault of stars—the entire universe beyond earth—to rotate out of position!

This troubling knowledge apparently was initially confined to a restricted circle of philosophers, and then became adopted by the elite of the Mediterranean city of Tarsus. Gradually, this knowledge spread as a cult of a new god, Mithras, who was powerful enough to shift the universe and abolish the previous home of the equinoctial sun, the constellation of Taurus. The appeal of such a religion can readily be understood: After all, adherents, if patient, were eventually introduced to what was literally one of the secrets of the universe!

This modern discovery of the basis of Mithraism explains a lot of its features. For example, some of the underground shrines to Mithras were punctured with small holes in the ceiling and walls. It is now thought that these holes may have pointed to certain stars or constellations (Ulansey, 1989, p. 17). Also, the figure of Mithras itself seems to have been derived from the constellation of the Greek hero, Perseus, positioned just above Taurus in the night sky. Perseus, like Mithras, is usually portrayed in ancient stellar maps as wearing a pointed hat. This hat, in fact, is the magical Cap of Hades that had been given to Perseus, and which allowed him to become invisible when fighting adversaries. In Greek mythology, the cap helped Perseus kill the Gorgon Medusa, whose horrible visage turned men to stone. To kill the Gorgon, Perseus had to avoid looking directly at her, and used her reflection in his shield to locate her. Similarly, Mithras is often portrayed as averting his eyes as he plunges his sword into the back of the bull. It seems likely that the god Mithras was actually Perseus; to disguise his identity and increase the exotic and esoteric aspects of the cult, he was given a name associated with both Perseus and with Persia by the ancient Greeks (Ulansey, 1989, p. 28).

The frequent depiction of the animals associated with the Zodiac in sculptures and paintings within Mithraic shrines is obviously connected with the astronomical basis of Mithraism. Not infrequently, some of these animals are portrayed as licking up the blood of the dying bull (Ulansey, 1989, p. 9 and 56). Also, in sculptures dating from between 100 B.C. to A.D. 250, ears of grain are often portrayed as sprouting from the bull's neck wound along with the blood (Ulansey, 1989, p. 56). This would seem to be an understandable reference to the coming of spring rains with the spring equinox that foster the growth of life-giving wheat. Justin Martyr, an ancient Christian writer, reported that Mithraic worshippers often partook of a meal of bread and wine mixed with water that symbolized eating the body and blood of the bull (Meyer, 1987, p. 199). Also, he was disturbed to note that the seven stages of Mithraic initiation correspond to the seven sacraments established by the early Church.

This recent illumination of the mysteries of the Mithraic cult is fascinating in itself. But, in addition, Mithraism has had an apparent impact upon the origins and practice of Christianity. St. Paul himself was a native of Tarsus and certainly was well acquainted with Mithraism. He and other early Christians had to compete with Mithraism to spread the Gospel. To effectively compete, early Christians appear to have made considerable efforts to appeal to the adherents of the rival religion. For example, in Mithraism, Sunday was held to be the sacred day of the sun. To compete with this day, early Christians appear to have shifted the

Sabbath away from the Jewish day of Saturday to Sunday. Another day sacred to Mithraism was December 25, which was only four days away from the winter solstice and supposedly the birthday of Mithras. Historical evidence suggests that the celebration of the birth of Christ was shifted to December 25 in the early centuries of Christianity (Baigent, 1996, p. 387; Fideler, 1989, p. 145). As Christianity gained greater prominence in the ancient world, Mithraism came under increasing attack, and was officially suppressed in Europe by the end of the fifth century.

An understanding of the precession of the equinoxes may not only help explain Mithraism, but may also explain the origin of the constellations of the Zodiac itself. Thousands of years ago, when the European Zodiac is thought to have originated, the spring equinox took place in Taurus, rather than in the present day Pisces. Conceivably, this could have symbolized the sun being tossed higher up into the sky by the horns of Taurus to initiate summer. At the summer solstice, the sun was in the constellation of Leo, the King of Beasts and Lord of a Hot Climate. At the autumnal equinox, the sun was being dragged downwards again by the claws of Scorpio, the Scorpion. Finally, the winter Mediterranean rains accompanying the winter solstice took place under the influence of Aquarius, the Water Carrier. At one point in time, the symbols of the Zodiac were in harmony with the seasons themselves. Due to the precession of the equinoxes, however, this symbolism has fallen out of synchrony with the seasons and is no longer so useful (Hawkins, 1983, p. 22).

There is evidence for a direct connection of Mithraic thought to Rennes-le-Chateau itself. This evidence was uncovered by Lynn Picknett and Clive Prince, who, while researching the area for their book on the Templars, examined a peculiar underground chamber present beneath the grounds of a medieval church close to Rennes-le-Chateau. The church is the basilica of Notre Dame de Marceille, located just north of Limoux, and at one time was a property of the Templars (Picknett, 1997, p. 197). The underground chamber appears to date from A.D. 200–300, and while generally neglected over the centuries, bears signs of having been used much more recently, and is equipped with a relatively modern iron gate that bars easy entrance into a tunnel from aboveground. Picknett and Prince speculated that this underground chamber at one time served as some sort of ceremonial site. In fact, this chamber has all the characteristics of a Mithraic shrine, in which ceremonies initiating newcomers into the cult were carried out. Dozens of such underground chambers are known to exist throughout Europe; the location of one of these in the area of Rennes-le-Chateau may be another example of a long-standing interest in the astronomical significance of this area (Picknett, 1997; Ulansey, 1989).

Although there is no direct evidence of a transmission of Mithraic thought to the Templars, many elements of Mithraism are apparent in some of the rites of Freemasonry, as noted above. Needless to say, the *content* of Mithraism (celebrating the killing of Taurus, the Bull) is absent from Freemasonry, but some of the *forms* of Mithraism seem preserved in Masonic customs. But is there any direct evidence that Masonry owes some of its symbolism to the Templars?

Some direct evidence of an early connection between the Templars and Freemasonry can be found at Roslyn, a chapel located just to the south of Edinburgh in Scotland. This stone chapel, constructed between 1440 and 1486 by Earl William St. Clair, contains many puzzling symbolic images carved in stone. The chapel contains fourteen freestanding stone columns. Twelve columns are identical to each other and are not particularly noteworthy; two remaining columns, however, are each highly carved and appear to represent the Masonic columns Jachin and Boaz. A carved image bearing a head wound appears to represent the Masonic figure of Hiram Abif. Also, a small carving actually depicts a Templar administering Masonic rites to an Entered Apprentice. (Knight, 1998, p. 301). Numerous Templar gravestones are associated with this chapel. The overall floor plan of the chapel closely matches the floor plan of the Temple of Solomon in Jerusalem, and apparently was meant to be a deliberate duplicate of it (Knight, 1997, p. 325). All this data supports the concept that many of the rituals of Freemasonry may have originated in the initiation rites of the Templars.

Astronomy and Other Medieval Monuments

There is additional evidence showing how a pre-Christian interest in the religious significance of astronomy was incorporated into religious sites and gradually absorbed, adopted, or repressed by Christianity. Some traces of this process can also be found in other locations in Europe. For example, in present-day Bosnia, dozens of sites can be found that contain stone monuments, or *stecaks,* created by a ninth-century religious sect called the Bogomils, derived from the Old Church Slavonic words for "God" and "merciful" or "dear" (Hristov, 1985). The most prominent collection of these monuments can be found in the vicinity of the town of Stolac, about forty miles northwest of Dubrovnik (Cuddon, 1974, p. 342). Many of these monuments show carved depictions of the sun and moon; they are located at precisely the same latitude as are Rennes-le-Chateau and Santiago de Compostela. The Bogomils are known to have communicated with the similar unorthodox religious community of Cathars near Rennes-le-Chateau (Baigent, 1996, p. 52). It is conceivable, though not proven, that some of the same astronomical themes found at Rennes-le-Chateau could have been shared by the Bogomils.

Curiously, a modern-day miracle, that of visions of the Virgin Mary, has been reported by village girls from the town of Medjugorje, thirty miles east of Stolac. The phenomenon made famous at the mountain village of Lourdes in France seems to have been repeated in another mountain village, at the same latitude, in Croatia.

Other puzzling artifacts, perhaps related both to astronomy and the Templars, can be found in southern France close to the latitude of Rennes-le-Chateau. One of these is located near the village of Falicon, ten kilometers to the northwest of the city of

Nice. Close to this mountaintop village, on a hillside called Aven des Ratapignata, an old, ten-foot-tall pyramid constructed out of stone blocks can be found (Tompkins, 1971, p. 140; see also a web page at www.beyond.fr/villages/falicon.html). This pyramid was constructed by Templars in the thirteenth century. According to an investigator named Maurice Guignaud, the pyramid is constructed so that at solar noon on September 21 (the autumnal equinox), the sun strikes it at an angle so that it casts no shadow on any side. The pyramid is built over two subterranean pits; the rock walls of these pits are inscribed with astronomical symbols suggesting it was used as some sort of astronomical observatory. Thus, the Templars constructed yet another astronomically significant structure, slightly north of the latitude of Rennes-le-Chateau, whose exact purpose is not yet understood.

It is curious that many of the structures we have been examining in this book—the churches at Rennes-le-Chateau, the major cathedral at Santiago de Compostela, the Templar castle at Ponferrada—were all constructed during the late eleventh or early twelfth centuries. If we assume that the construction of these structures was at least partly guided by an interest in astronomical events, is there any explanation why astronomy might have had a renewed popularity during this time?

In fact, an unusual astronomical event did indeed take place in A.D. 1054. This was a gigantic explosion of a large star that created a suddenly visible "new star" or supernova. Modern astronomers have examined the remnants of this titanic explosion, one of only a few that take place every thousand years in our own galaxy. This explosion created the Crab Nebula, located in the constellation of Taurus—the same constellation that had been of such interest to the Mithraic cult six hundred years earlier. This supernova was so bright that it was visible during the day for a month and remained as bright as the moon for an entire year (Krupp, 1995; *Washington Post,* 1996, p. A3).

We know of the characteristics of this supernova because it was recorded in five different reports written by Chinese and Japanese astronomers in that year that have survived. The Crab Nebula supernova was apparently also visible to an observer in Baghdad, Ibn Butlan, and may have been recorded in stone carvings by American Indians (Krupp, 1995). As yet, no written reactions to this new star by European observers have been found. However, we can assume that this event was noted in Europe just as in other parts of the world. We know that Europeans of the time did observe heavenly events, since the appearance of Halley's comet in A.D. 1066 was depicted with some wonderment in the Bayeux tapestry, an embroidered record of the Norman conquest of England (Ley, 1963, p. 150). The description of a later and dimmer supernova in 1572 helped start the illustrious career of the early astronomer, Tycho Brahe (Ley, 1963, p. 85). So, this astronomical event may have conceivably rekindled interest in the astronomical monuments and inclinations of earlier Europeans.

CHAPTER 10

Astronomy at Other
Templar and Masonic Sites

OUTSIDE OF THE MAIN AREAS FOCUSED UPON IN THIS book, there are additional sites that show how interested Templar and later Masonic organizations were in astronomy. One of these, a small Danish island called Bornholm, has been described in some detail by Henry Lincoln and co-authors (Haagensen, 2000; Lincoln, 1997, p. 181).

The number of puzzling phenomena present on Bornholm is surprising for an island of such a small size. One outstanding feature is the presence of almost a thousand megalithic standing stones, mainly present along the northern coast (Haagensen, 2000, p. 9). Since megalithic constructions are relatively rarer in Scandinavia as compared to more southern European locations, this unexpected concentration of megalithic stones is of interest to us in the context of megalithic astronomy.

In addition, a collection of fifteen medieval churches can be found on Bornholm; four of these show the cylindrical (round wall) architecture characteristic of Templar churches, and are associated with rock carvings that depict the Templar cross (Haagensen, 2000, p. 13). The churches were constructed at the end of the twelfth century. At about the same time (A.D. 1171), Pope Alexander III proclaimed a long-awaited Crusade against marauding pagans in nearby Estonia. Contingents of the Knights Templar appear to have been called to Denmark and Bornholm to lend their military might to the Crusade, and the fortified Templar churches were constructed to provide both spiritual and physical security for the Knights. According to Haagensen and Lincoln, the geographical placement of these churches on Bornholm gives evidence of a meticulous construction of a geometric design somewhat reminiscent of that present in Rennes-le-Chateau (Fig. 17).

The largest church, Østerlars, is located in an exact geometric relationship to two other churches, Nylars and Rutsker (the suffix "ker" corresponds to the German "kirche" or Scottish "kirk" and denotes a church). Both churches are located precisely 14,336 meters from Østerlars with an accuracy amounting to only a four-inch difference between Østerlars-Rutsker and Østerlars-Nylars (Haagensen, 2000, p. 50). This suggests that Østerlars occupies the center of a huge circle that intersects the positions of Nylars and Rutsker. Also, the line connecting Nylars with Østerlars accurately points to stone structures on another small island (Christiansø) miles away from Bornholm, and suggests a major axis through the

Fig. 17
Locations of Templar Churches on the Island of Bornholm

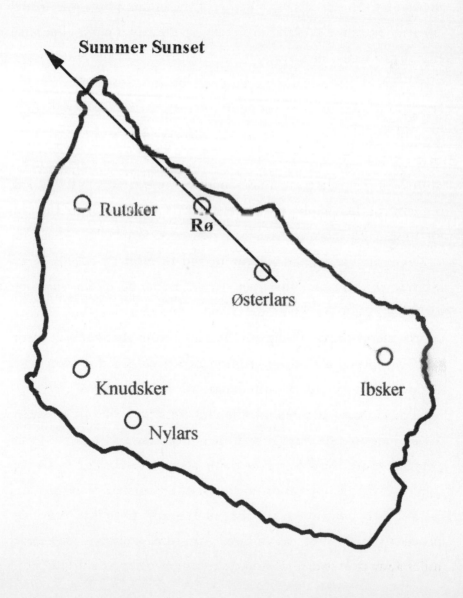

circle around Østerlars. Haagensen and Lincoln propose that this circle around Østerlars and the line through it form the basis for huge five- and six-pointed star-shaped geometrical figures that are anchored to the positions of many of the churches on the island. Their book tells a complicated story of measurement and geometry that is well worth reading.

However, the astronomical aspects of their story are of more immediate interest to us. In addition to forming the center of a gigantic circle, the Østerlars church also appeared to be used as an astronomical observatory. The church consists of a round stone rotunda surrounding an inner circular stone tower. Narrow, slit windows in the circular tower are aligned with similar windows in the rotunda to allow a narrow view of the exterior. One such pair of windows was deliberately positioned to permit the passage of the rays of the rising sun only on the morning of the summer solstice (Haagensen, 2000, p. 52 and 131). This suggests that the church incorporated a long-standing interest in astronomy. Is there anything special about the location of Bornholm that would be dictated by astronomical considerations?

The latitude of Bornholm (about 55 degrees N) is between the latitudes of Stonehenge and the isle of Lewis; from what I can calculate using SkyMap Pro, there appears to be a 90-degree angle between the positions of the setting sun and rising sun on the horizon on the day of the winter solstice at the maximal standstill point of the moon during its 18.6 year cycle (see Table 4). This certainly does not occur routinely at most sites, though many calculations at many latitudes would be necessary to show that this is unique to Bornholm. Was this unusual event of interest to the creators of the Templar churches on Bornholm?

Table 4

Lunar and Solar Locations at the Maximum Standstill Point of the Full Moon at the latitude of Bornholm

Summer Solstice, 2006

Full Moonrise	148 degrees from true north
Full Moonset	216 degrees
Sunrise	45 degrees
Sunset	315 degrees

Winter Solstice, 2006

Full Moonrise	36 degrees
Full Moonset	323 degrees
Sunrise	136 degrees
Sunset	226 degrees

A comparison of the positions of the sun and moon during the summer solstice with the locations of churches around Østerlars does provide an interesting correlation. One church, Rø, is located at an angle of 316 degrees away from Østerlars, approximately the position of the setting sun at the summer solstice. This church is located about 5400 meters away from Østerlars. Rø is also located on a straight line that runs from another church (Klemensker) and the island of Christiansø. The evident use of Østerlars as an astronomical observatory, together with the positioning of these other churches, strongly suggests, but does not prove, that the placement of these structures may have been based upon an earlier preoccupation with geometry and astronomy, as in other European sites.

If this is true, what other European sites can we examine to explore the astronomy of the latitude of Bornholm further? This question would not seem easy to answer, at first. Except for Bornholm itself and small portions of Denmark, the 55th parallel at the longitude of Europe mainly cuts across miles of empty ocean, which leaves no signature of human activity. However, the 55th parallel does cover the northernmost part of Ireland and northwest England. Is there anything of interest at these locations?

In fact, these particular portions of Ireland and England are noteworthy for possessing unusually numerous examples of megalithic stones aligned in rows. According to Aubrey Burl, the paramount expert on prehistoric stone rows in Europe, there are about 170 examples of long, single rows of megalithic stones buried in the ground in Ireland, England, and Brittany in France. Most of these, however, are not scattered randomly throughout these countries, but are concentrated in four major sites: Northern Ireland at Beaghmore, just south of Londonderry; northwestern England, at Shap, just south of Carlisle; Culbone Hill in southwestern England (at the latitude of Stonehenge); and scattered along the coast of Brittany (Burl, 1993, p. 92).

In Ireland, about 130 megalithic stone circles have been described. These stone circles are also not randomly located throughout the island. Fifty-five of these stone circles are found within fifty miles of Londonderry, and most of the remainder (seventy-seven) are clustered in a small area far to the south at the latitude of Cork (Brennan, 1994, p. 21). These data show that only specific latitudes in the United Kingdom are enriched in megalithic structures.

The two sites in Beaghmore (Ireland) and near Carlisle (England) are of particular interest to us, since they both are located at a latitude of 54° 40', just a few miles south of the latitude of Dornholm. Beaghmore (Gaelic for "great birches") was first excavated in 1945; large quantities of peat had to be removed to reveal many of the smaller megalithic stones located at this site in County Tyrone. Carbon-14 dating of organic material found beneath some of the stones suggests that the stones were erected some time between 2100-1600 B.C., i.e., at a time roughly similar to the period of construction of Stonehenge in England. The arrangement of stone circles at Beaghmore is rather unusual: Three pairs of closely adjacent stone circles, rather than individual circles, were constructed (Burl, 1993, p. 106). Is it possible that this was a deliberate choice to commemorate the two positions of the sun on the horizon during the solstice?

In addition to stone circles, there are six long rows of stones, plus two smaller rows, at Beaghmore. In 1980, Dr. Archie Thom, Alexander Thom's son, surveyed these rows to examine their possible astronomical orientations. One of the long rows of stones is oriented at 45 degrees from true north, an angle which would point at the rising sun at the summer solstice. Astronomical orientations of the other rows are not so clearly understood. One complication arises from evidence that the area had once been more heavily forested than it is today. This would have resulted in an elevation of the horizon by almost 3 degrees in ancient times. If this factor is corrected for, four of the other stone rows show a rough alignment with the setting sun at the winter solstice (Burl, 1993, p. 105).

The collection of megalithic sites just south of Carlisle, in England, is also of interest. One prominent site is a huge stone circle located at Penrith. This circle is one of the largest in England, having a diameter of almost 360 feet, three times the diameter of Stonehenge. It is composed of a circle of sixty-seven stones adjacent to two larger stones that each weigh thirty tons and would have required the effort of one hundred men to move and position. These larger stones seem to represent a "doorway" into the circle. Further away from these stones, an even larger stone called "Long Meg" is located. The line between Long Meg and the "doorway" stones points precisely to the setting sun during the winter solstice.

This region of England, like many others, contains a stone Temple erected by the Knights Templar in Sowerby, four miles east of Penrith and just south of the Long Meg group.

It is not unreasonable to conclude that these stone constructions in England and Ireland were also constructed at an astronomically significant latitude, like the stone circles at Stonehenge and the island of Lewis (see Chapter 1). Thus, the evidence of interest in astronomy present in the structures at Bornholm seems to be repeated in the megalithic structures at the same latitude in the British Isles.

As we have seen, many of the important megalithic sites in Europe—at Callanish, Beaghmore, Bornholm, Stonehenge, Carnac, and Rennes-le-Chateau—are constructed at precisely the latitudes needed to observe astronomical events involving the sun and moon (See Table 5).

One final feature present on Bornholm is of interest to us. A fresco on an interior wall in Nyker church depicts the Lamb of God, surrounded by painted stars and bleeding profusely from a wound in its neck. A cup, presumably the Holy Grail, is positioned to collect the blood flowing from the wound (Haagensen, 2000, p. 117). This portrayal, while unusual, is not generally inconsistent with Christian orthodoxy, but it does show a remarkable resemblance to Mithraic portrayals of Taurus, the Bull, bleeding from the knife wound in the shoulder, with animals of the Zodiac lapping up the blood. Perhaps this is another indication of a hidden meaning of Templar symbolism that leads to their occult knowledge of pre-Christian astronomical faiths.

Astronomical and Masonic Sites in the United States

If we accept that Templar interests were inherited or adopted by the Freemasons, then several sites linked to Masonry outside of Europe also reveal a link with astronomy. One site is located near

the town of Kilmarnock, in Lancaster County, Virginia, southeast
of Washington, D.C. and not far from the Chesapeake Bay. A
church at this site called Christ Church displays some curious
astronomical orientations (*Richmond Times-Dispatch,* April 23,
2000; Taylor, 1997). This brick church was erected on the site of
an earlier church, built in 1670 and replaced in 1735. It is oriented 3½ degrees away from an east–west axis. This positioning
allows a beam of sunlight to pass through an oval window placed
over the west door and illuminate the altar only two times a year:
Once about fourteen days after the vernal equinox, which is in
the middle of the Easter season, and 180 days later, during the
time of the autumnal equinox. A number of other structural features also point to a preoccupation with astronomy and divisions
of the year: 1) the church is cruciform in shape and has twelve
walls and twelve windows, equal in number to the months of the
year, 2) there are twenty-six pews in the church, equal to half the
number of weeks in a year, and 3) there are twenty-six panels in
the west door.

This church has been intensely investigated by a local amateur
astronomer, Stephen Stewart, who discovered the positioning of
the sunbeam at Easter entirely by accident in 1988. Stewart spec-
ulates that the plan of the church may have been adapted from a
design by the distinguished English architect Sir Christopher
Wren, who was believed to have been a Freemason and who
once taught astronomy at Oxford. Christ Church has many
architectural similarities to Farley church in Surrey, England,

just south of London, which was restored by Christopher Wren and which at one time also possessed a circular window over its main entrance door.

Funds for the church were provided by Robert "King" Carter, an extremely wealthy owner of a large tobacco plantation in eastern Virginia. Carter's ancestors had immigrated from England in the 1680s and maintained their connection to the mother country. Carter himself was educated in England and had an opportunity to observe many buildings designed by Wren to replace those lost in the Great Fire of London. While Carter probably did not design Christ Church himself, he may have employed an architect who adapted Wren's design. Carter, who came to own 300,000 acres and 1,000 slaves, died in 1732 and was buried in an aboveground tomb on the grounds of his new church. His tomb is inscribed with a skull and crossbones, a symbol that is often, though not exclusively, associated with Freemasonry.

Whatever the explanation, the form of the church is an undeniable expression of an interest in astronomy that was carried from Europe to the colonies long ago. It also serves to remind us that Easter and Passover are linked to an astronomical event—the vernal equinox—that was central to Mithraic thinking.

Finally, yet another surprising connection between the Masons and astronomy actually seems apparent in the overall plan for Washington, D. C., itself. Evidence for this connection has been presented in detail in a book by David Ovason (Ovason, 2000, pp. 45 and 261).

The general plan for the city was created, at the suggestion of George Washington, by two architects, the Frenchman Pierre Charles L'Enfant and the American Andrew Ellicott in 1791. One striking feature of this plan was the novel introduction of diagonal boulevards in the city, the most prominent one being Pennsylvania Avenue. The reasons behind this novel plan are uncertain, but L'Enfant may have taken some inspiration from the plans of an architect who might have been connected with the design of Christ Church: Christopher Wren, the astronomer and suspected Freemason who had also incorporated boulevards radiating from principal points into his plan for the rebuilding of London after the Great Fire in the 1660s (Bryan, 1914, p. 142).

Pennsylvania Avenue was designed to provide a direct view of the White House from the Capitol building, thus symbolizing the interaction between the Executive and Legislative branches of government. Pennsylvania Avenue also forms one side of a large right triangle that includes the Mall along one long side and a line passing through the area of the Washington Monument on the short side of the triangle. These are well-known features of the capital city.

What has not been recognized is that Pennsylvania Avenue also seems oriented to align with an astronomical event. An observer at the Capitol building looking down Pennsylvania Avenue on the evening of August 10 will see the sun setting at the end of the avenue only on that day. About half an hour later, this same spot on the horizon marks the setting of a significant constellation, which

Fig. 18
Astronomy of the Federal Triangle

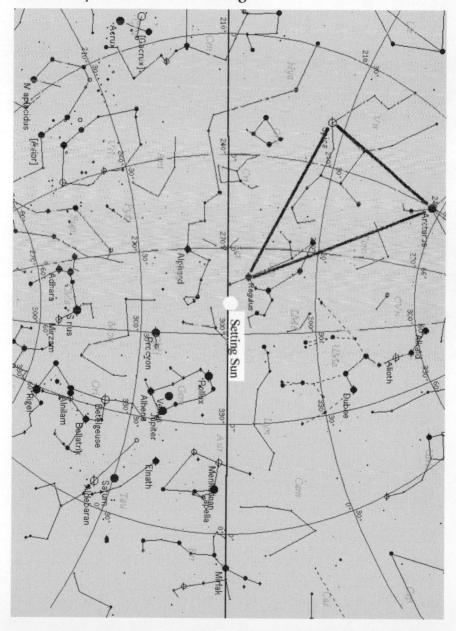

is known but not easily seen at this time because of the lingering brightness in the night sky. The stars that set at this site include those of the constellation Virgo, which has a role in many examples of Masonic symbolism, and which is also identified with the Virgin Mary. Surrounding this constellation is a right triangle formed by three first magnitude (very bright) stars, Regulus, Arcturus, and Spica. The general form of this triangle mimics the form of the Federal Triangle formed by Pennsylvania and Constitution Avenues (Ovason, 2000, p. 347) (Fig. 18). Ovason has proposed that the Federal Triangle was oriented and constructed to commemorate a comparable triangle in the night sky.

As was mentioned in Chapter 3, a right triangle analogous to the Federal Triangle in Washington, D.C., can be traced out on the ground near Rennes-le-Chateau by drawing lines between structures at Blanchefort, Arques, and Peyrolles. This triangle also points toward Regulus and the stellar triangle enclosing the constellation Virgo. The Federal Triangle, in addition to being oriented to the sun setting near Regulus, also has another feature in common with the triangle marked out on the ground at Rennes-le-Chateau. Pennsylvania Avenue strikes an angle from true north that amounts to precisely 288 degrees, when measured clockwise from the true north, as is the convention. However, when measured counterclockwise from true north, this angle equals 72 degrees, the pentagonal angle present at Rennes-le-Chateau. Thus, the Federal Triangle represents a mirror image of the triangle at Rennes-le-Chateau, pointing at the August setting sun in the west rather than at the rising sun to the east. This angle is required for this particular orientation toward Regulus. None of the other diagonal boulevards in Washington, D.C., follow this precise angle. Thus, it seems possible that the orientation of Pennsylvania Avenue toward Regulus may have been intentional. It hardly seems likely that these similar triangles oriented toward the same point in the sky could both be coincidental. These two triangles, constructed hundreds of years apart, may be reasonable evidence of the preservation of an astronomical symbolism throughout the centuries by the Knights Templar and their spiritual descendents, the Freemasons.

How can we evaluate this hypothesis? The validity of Ovason's proposal might be easier to examine if the astronomical object that he discusses were more distinctive. For example, the contention by John North that the "Long Man" figure cut into the turf in East Sussex represents the constellation Orion seems hard to refute: Orion does indeed rise above this figure, and there are no other bright constellations in the sky that approximate a man-shaped pattern (see Chapter 1). If the designers of Washington, D.C., had elected to create a representation of the Big Dipper on the ground that pointed to the same constellation in the sky, a connection between the design of Washington, D.C., and astronomy would be hard to deny. But many triangles between the abundant stars of the night sky can be constructed. Is it possible that the Federal Triangle points to the Regulus triangle just by chance? How prominent is the Regulus-Arcturus-Spica triangle in the night sky?

To examine Ovason's proposal, it would be helpful to experience the impact of the stellar triangle firsthand. This triangle is easily seen on star charts (Fig. 18), but this abstract knowledge about the star formation does not directly tell us how powerful an influence this triangle might have had upon the imaginations of the architects of Washington, D.C. The night sky in those days, before gas or electric light, provided a much greater spectacle than it does now to us modern city dwellers. In fact, very few constellations can now be seen above Pennsylvania Avenue at night, since it is too well-lit to permit a good view of the night sky.

To overcome this problem, my wife and I drove fifty miles west of Washington, D.C., to Sky Meadows State Park, near Paris (!), Virginia. Each month in this park, astronomers from the Air and Space Museum of the Smithsonian Institution hold an informal seminar on astronomy for the public. The park is ideal for this purpose: It is located in the foothills of the Blue Ridge Mountains, far from large towns. The grassy area of the park is surrounded by hills that block any light from nearby streets and which form a natural amphitheater very similar to an artificial planetarium. With the sun set, and in the absence of a full moon, this park is the darkest place I have ever experienced—we both had to take special care not to collide in the dark with other enthusiasts attending the talk. The only illumination allowed was from small flashlights dimmed with red cellophane covers to facilitate our eyes' adaptation to the dark.

However, the long drive and the dark were certainly worth it, and I highly recommend it to you, the reader. The brilliance of the constellations under these conditions certainly did not disappoint. And sure enough, the Regulus–Spica–Arcturus triangle was one of the most noteworthy features of the night sky. Arcturus is particularly easy to identify. If you can locate the Big Dipper, find the curved "handle" of the Dipper, which describes a brief "arc." Follow the curve of this "arc" to the left of the Big Dipper and you will quickly see the very bright star Arcturus (Fig. 18). If you have access to any reasonably dark environment, this exercise is worth pursuing. This experience was enough to satisfy me that inhabitants of the newly created American capital, poorly lighted and sparsely populated, could not have failed to note the triangle Ovason has described.

Another objection to Ovason's proposal might be that the influence of the Masons and esoteric Masonic thought would be too feeble to dictate the very foundations of the new American capital. However, anyone making such an objection would only be showing an ignorance of the importance of the Masonic movement in the early history of the United States. A great proportion of the signers of the Declaration of Independence were Masons, and the Masonic ideals of brotherhood and equality appear to have had an enormous influence in Revolutionary times. George Washington was a lifelong Mason and was a member of Alexandria Lodge Number 22, founded in 1783. The influence of the Masons continued into the first years of the new republic. When

Andrew Ellicott had completed his initial surveying of the boundaries of the future District of Columbia, the first cornerstone of the District boundary was laid on March 15, 1794, at Jones Point south of Alexandria by a detachment of Masons, who afterward retired to speeches and refreshment at the nearby Wise's tavern (Bryan, 1914, p. 143). In 1795, the Washington Lodge of Masons observed the Sabbath on June 24 (St. John's day) in a building adjacent to the new Capitol Building (Bryan, 1914, p. 261). Ovason, however, does not provide documentary evidence that Ellicott or L'Enfant were members of any Masonic lodge.

Numerous other buildings, symbols, and monuments in and around Washington, D. C., show a continuing connection to Masonry. For example, when construction on the Washington Monument was resumed in 1880, Masons laid a cornerstone at exactly 10:59 A.M., a time at which the star Virgo rises above the horizon (Ovason, 2000, p. 131). The Washington Monument itself, of course, is modeled after an Egyptian obelisk, another symbol often utilized by Freemasonry. A memorial statue to the assassinated President Garfield, a prominent Mason, was designed and erected close to the Capitol in 1887 by a Freemason, John Quincy Adams Ward; this statue contains a Zodiac and numerous examples of Masonic symbolism (Ovason, 2000, p. 207). The Great Seal of the United States, displayed on the back of each dollar bill, shows a pyramid surmounted by the All-Seeing Eye, which is another mystic Masonic symbol. A continuing Masonic tradition of astronomical symbolism may explain the remarkable number of

Zodiacs displayed throughout the city on monuments, statues, and even in the Dirksen Senate Office Building.

Perhaps the most dramatic example of a Masonic structure in the Washington area is the George Washington National Masonic Memorial building in nearby Alexandria. This building, completed in 1932 thanks to voluntary donations from Masons throughout the United States, is a 333-foot-high stone tower that overlooks the city from a hill. On display within it is a seventeen-foot-tall bronze statue of George Washington, Masonic paraphernalia owned by Washington, a sword once owned by a Templar knight from medieval Germany, and rooms decorated with Egyptian and other esoteric symbols (see www.gwmemorial.org). The influence of Masons in American government continues: To date, fourteen Presidents, eight Vice Presidents, and forty-two Supreme Court Justices have been Masons. However, the story of Masonry in the United States is not one of unbroken ascension to greater and greater influence. Nothing illustrates the ups and downs of Masonry better than the sequence of events that took place in the 1820s.

The early decades of the nineteenth century saw the foundation of a vigorous Anti-Mason movement in the United States. The impetus for this development was the announcement by a former Mason, William Morgan of Batavia, N.Y., that he planned to publish a book detailing the secret ceremonies and handshakes of the Masons. Shortly afterward Morgan was kidnapped and was never seen again. Years later, a Mason named Henry Valance confessed on his deathbed to killing Morgan. When Morgan's book was published posthumously in 1827, a great public uproar protesting Morgan's disappearance and fulminating against the rites and secrets of Masonry began. This resulted in the formation of America's first third party, the Antimasons, which held a political convention in Philadelphia in 1830 and polled 128,000 votes, a very respectable number considering the small voting population of the time (Marrs, 2000, p. 217; Muzzey, 1927, p. 361). One of the goals of the party was to unseat Andrew Jackson, himself a Mason, and to purge the government of the large numbers of Masons who held positions of influence. This political movement had a disastrous effect upon the activity and membership rolls of Freemasonry for years afterward. Jackson, however, withstood the efforts of his enemies to remove him from office and eventually the party diverted its interests to other issues and dwindled or merged with the Whig party.

One paradoxical effect of this political movement was that many university fraternities found the somber rituals of Freemasonry to be appealing. University students appear to have blithely appropriated these newly revealed mysteries for their own initiation rites. An important example of a university society utilizing some of the signs of Masonry is the Yale fraternity Skull and Bones, founded in 1832 by General William H. Russell and Alphonso Taft of Cincinnati, who had served in the Rutherford Hayes administration as Attorney General. Russell apparently based his organization upon the rules of a German university society he had become acquainted with during his stay in Germany. For this reason, he called his society chapter 2 of Skull and Bones, and the official Bones badge worn by initiates displayed a Skull with the number 322 (for 1832, chapter 2) positioned below the skull in place of the jaw. Skull and Bones still meets in a windowless brownstone building near the campus of Yale University and uses a number of secret initiation rites that somewhat resemble those of Freemasonry.

Since many Yale students come from highly placed families, and since Skull and Bones recruits from among the most influential and wealthy students, many extremely prominent Americans were once Bones men: President William H. Taft (Alphonso Taft's son), Presidents George H. W. Bush, and George W. Bush, Prescott Bush, Percy Rockefeller, Averill Harriman, McGeorge Bundy, Henry Luce, and William F. Buckley are all examples of Bones men (Marrs, 2000, p. 90; Stevens, 1907, p. 179). Some authors have darkly speculated that the Skull and Bones and the Masons exert a hidden, conspiratorial influence upon American government (Marrs, p. 90, 2000). It seems unlikely that some sort of conspiracy is the actual goal of these organizations, but Skull and Bones and the Masons do offer opportunities for influential individuals to socialize, get to know each other, and subsequently coordinate their goals and ideas.

Conclusion

It is fair to say that the bulk of this book has been concerned with two main themes: the detection of patterns (in nature and in history) and the assignment of meaning to these patterns.

These activities are of course primary functions of human intelligence. Without them, life would be a continuous succession of random, meaningless events.

The first patterns we discussed were the movements of the sun and moon, detected by the creators of prehistoric megalithic monuments. We can only guess that these patterns were observed in prehistory by, once again, discerning an astronomical pattern in the arrangement of stones left behind by these cultures. Since the people who created these monuments never left records explaining them, we can only infer a meaning from the placement of the stones. The new observation made in this book that megalithic monuments are particularly elaborate and numerous at latitudes with astronomical significance may suggest that a common observational and philosophical system existed throughout Europe. This assertion is reasonable, but not indisputable. We can't go back through time to find an absolutely correct answer.

The second pattern we have discussed is the relationship of Templar castles to these astronomically oriented megalithic sites. It is clear that numerous structures created by the Knights Templar are located near megalithic sites dedicated to astronomy (Avebury-Stonhenge, Aachen, Carnac, Rennes-le-Chateau, Ponferrada, Santiago de Compostela, Falicon, Penrith and Bornholm). At the very least, the locations of these Templar structures show that the Templars were aware of the existence of the nearby megalithic sites. Many of these Templar structures are part of an array of structures aligned with the setting sun or moon, or else show inscriptions or structural features that betray an interest in astronomy. The question is: Did the Templars know the significance of the specific latitudes of these places, which made these sites sacred places of worship of the cosmos in pre-Christian times? The secretive and hierarchical society of the Knights Templar left few written records that could illuminate this question. What other evidence shows that the Templars knew of the religious significance of astronomical events?

If we accept the argument that Freemasonry originated much earlier than is commonly accepted, and acquired some of its features from the Knights Templar—and I think the evidence presented in this book makes this argument a reasonable one then some of the features of Freemasonry can be utilized in an attempt to further understand the Templars. The obvious connections of the rites of Freemasonry with those of ancient Mithraism, and the numerous references to astronomical subjects in Freemasonry do suggest that the antecedents of the Masons did indeed have a sophisticated understanding of the philosophical meanings of astronomical events. Such knowledge should not be too surprising.

The Knights Templar were established to fight for Christendom and to rescue the souls of the pagans they encountered, both in the Middle East and in Europe itself. They took on this assignment at a time when Spain was in the grip of Muslims, when heretical societies like the Cathars still flourished, and when portions of Eastern Europe were still completely pagan. In order to expand the influence of Christianity, it was undoubtedly necessary to understand, and even partially accommodate, the conflicting philosophical ideas of their opponents. An attempt to incorporate pre-Christian, astronomically oriented religious practices into a peculiar amalgam of paganism and Christianity may likely have arisen from the efforts of the Templars.

There has been endless speculation about whether or not the Templars were in possession of a body of secret knowledge or of a hoard of treasure that escaped detection and is still awaiting discovery. One Templar secret that now does seem clear is that they knew that many of the sites and symbols honored by Christianity originated with, and were revered by, ancient peoples who worshipped astronomical events. This knowledge alone, in an epoch dominated by Christian orthodoxy, was dangerous and demanded secrecy.

One advantage of an astronomical theme in religious practices is that it makes it possible for any individual to have direct contact with the sacred. All anyone needs to observe a special alignment of the sun and moon, as at Stonehenge or Rennes-le-Chateau, is the necessary knowledge and the patience to wait. Perhaps the Cathars, the Templars, and those who came after them sought out this direct experience of a religious mystery. A direct observation of the sun and moon, or contact with a religious relic such as the Holy Grail or the Shroud of Turin, allows any person, regardless of rank or training, to have a holy experience without the need for a church hierarchy or an orthodox explanation of dogma or scripture. This arrangement was certainly what appears to have been sought by the Cathars, the Templars, or even the freethinking liberals of the Freemasons.

The disadvantage of an astronomical theme in religion is that it provides no moral or ethical guidelines, defines no virtues or sins, and cannot offer salvation or punishment. While astronomy can unlock some secrets of the universe, it provides no key to the human heart, and provides no ethical guidelines for human behavior. The absence of the human element in astronomically-oriented philosophies may have elevated them so far above the human level that they proved inadequate for humans. Perhaps this was one reason why Christianity eventually overcame the attractions of astronomy and led to the abandonment and oblivion of these associated sacred sites in Europe.

Table 5
Astronomical Basis for the Locations of Major Megalithic Constructions

Location of megalithic monuments	Latitude	Astronomical event occurring at the summer solstice
Callanish (Isle of Lewis)	57.2° N	Arctic circle for the moon (moon barely rises above the horizon)
Beaghmore (Ireland) Bornholm (Denmark)	55.0° N	Setting sun–rising sun angle equals 90 degrees
Aachen (Germany) Stonehenge (England)	51.1° N	Setting moon–setting sun angle equals exactly 90 degrees
Carnac (France)	47.6° N	Setting moon–rising moon angle equals exactly 90 degrees
Rennes-le-Chateau (France) Santiago de Compostela (Spain)	42.6° N	Rising sun–rising moon angle equals exactly 72 degrees

Fig. 19
Locations of Templar Churches on the Island of Bornholm

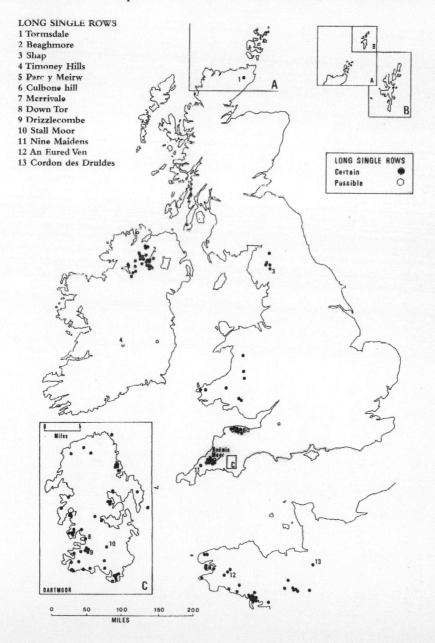

LONG SINGLE ROWS
1 Tormsdale
2 Beaghmore
3 Shap
4 Timoney Hills
5 Parc y Meirw
6 Culbone hill
7 Merrivale
8 Down Tor
9 Drizzlecombe
10 Stall Moor
11 Nine Maidens
12 An Eured Ven
13 Cordon des Druldes

LONG SINGLE ROWS
Certain   ●
Pussible   ○

Bibliography

Alberi, Mary. "Alcuin and the New Athens" *History Today* vol. 39:35–41, 1989.

Anderson, R. R., and Parrish, J. A. "The Optics of Human Skin" *Journal of Investigative Dermatology* vol. 77, pp. 13–19, 1981.

Andrews, R., and Schellenberger, P. *The Tomb of God.* New York: Little, Brown & Co., 1996.

Apostolos-Cappadona, Diane. *Dictionary of Christian Art.* New York: Continuum Publ. Co., 1994.

Atienza, Juan G. *Guía de la España templaria.* Barcelona: Editorial Ariel, S.A., 1985.

Baigent, M., Leigh, R., and Lincoln, H. *The Messianic Legacy.* New York: Dell Books, 1986.

Baigent, M., and Leigh, R. *The Temple and the Lodge.* New York: Arcade Publishing, 1989.

Baigent, M., Leigh, R., and Lincoln, H. *The Holy Blood and the Holy Grail.* London: Arrow Books, 1996.

Bentley, P. J. *Comparative Vertebrate Endocrinology.* New York: Cambridge Univ. Press, 1982.

Bernal, Martin. *Black Athena: The Afroasiatic Roots of Classical Civilization: Vol. 1 The Fabrication of Ancient Greece 1785-1985.* New York: Rutgers Univ. Press, 1991.

Bless, R. C. *Discovering the Cosmos.* Sausalito: University Science Books, 1996.

Brennan, Martin. *The Stones of Time: Calendars, Sundials, and Stone*

Chambers of Ancient Ireland. Rochester, VT: Inner Traditions, 1994.

Brown, Peter L. *Megaliths, Myths, and Men. An Introduction to Astro-Archaeology.* Mineola, N.Y.: Dover Publications, 1976.

Bryan, Wilhelmus. *A History of the National Capital. From Its Foundation through the Period of the Adoption of the Organic Act.* New York: MacMillan Co., 1914, Vol. 2.

Burl, Aubrey. *From Carnac to Callanish: The Prehistoric Stone Rows and Avenues of Britain, Ireland, and Brittany.* New York: Yale Univ. Press, 1993.

Campbell, Leroy. *Mithraic Iconography and Ideology.* Leiden: E. J. Brill, 1968.

Clayton, Peter. *Chronicle of the Pharaohs. The Reign-by-Reign Record of the Rulers and Dynasties of Ancient Egypt.* London: Thames & Hudson, 1994.

Churchill, Winston. *A History of the English-Speaking Peoples. Vol. 1. The Birth of Britain.* New York: Dodd, Mead, & Co., 1958.

Crow, John. *Spain: The Root and the Flower: An Interpretation of Spain and the Spanish People.* San Francisco: Univ. of California Press, 1985.

Cuddon, John. *The Companion Guide to Jugoslavia.* London: Collins, 1974.

Cyclopedia of American Biography. Ann Arbor, Michigan: Univ. Microfilms Press, vol. 16, 1967.

Dixon, W. J., and Massey, Jr., F. J. *Introduction to Statistical Analysis.* New York: McGraw-Hill, 1969.

Eisenman, Robert. *James the Brother of Jesus. The Key to Unlocking the Secrets of Early Christianity and the Dead Sea Scrolls.* New York: Viking, 1997.

Fideler, David. *Jesus Christ, Sun of God. Ancient Cosmology and Early Christian Symbolism.* Wheaton, IL: Quest Books, 1989.

Fletcher, R. A. *Saint James's Catapult. The Life and Times of Diego Gelmirez of Santiago de Compostela.* Oxford: Clarendon Press, 1984.

Gardner, Laurence. *The Bloodline of the Holy Grail: the Hidden Lineage of Jesus Revealed.* Rockport, MA: Element Publ., 1998.

Gibson, Walter S. *Hieronymus Bosch.* London: Thames & Hudson, 1973.

Gordon, Richard. *Image and Value in the Graeco-Roman World—Studies in Mithraism and Religious Art.* Vermont: Ashgate Publ., 1996.

Gowing, Lawrence. *Paintings of the Louvre.* New York: Stewart, Tabori, & Chang, 1987.

Gugliotti, Guy. "Stone Box May Be Oldest Link to Jesus" *Washington Post,* Oct. 22, 2002, p. A1.

Guyton, Arthur C. *Textbook of Medical Physiology.* Philadelphia: W. B. Saunders, 1971.

Haagensen, E., and Lincoln, H. *The Templars' Secret Island: the Knights, the Priest and the Treasure.* Moreton in Marsh: Windrush Press, 2000.

Hancock, G., and Bauval, R. *The Message of the Sphinx: A Quest for the Hidden Legacy of Mankind.* New York: Crown Publishers, 1996.

Hastings, James. *Encyclopedia of Religion and Ethics.* New York: Charles Scribners & Sons, 1922.

Hastings, Selina. *Evelyn Waugh: A Biography.* London: Sinclair-Stevens, 1994.

Hawkins, Gerald. *Stonehenge Decoded.* New York: Doubleday, 1965.

Hawkins, Gerald. *Mindsteps to the Cosmos.* New York: Harper & Row, 1983.

Heckethorn, Charles. *The Secret Societies of All Ages and Countries.* New York: University Books, 1965.

Herner, Russell A. *Stonehenge: An Ancient Masonic Temple.* Richmond, VA.: McCoy Publ. & Masonic Supply Co., 1984.

Hitt, Jack. *Off the Road: A Modern-day Walk Down the Pilgrim's Route into Spain.* New York: Simon & Schuster, 1989.

Howarth, Stephen. *The Knights Templar.* New York: Atheneum, 1982.

Hristov, Hristo. *A History of Bulgaria.* Sofia: Sofia Press, 1985.

King, Henry. *Pictorial Guide to the Stars.* New York: Thomas Y. Crowell Co., 1967.

Knight, C., and Lomas, R. *The Hiram Key—Pharaohs, Freemasons, and the Discovery of the Secret Scrolls of Jesus.* Boston: Element Books, 1997.

Knight, C. and Lomas, R. *The Second Messiah: the Templars, the Turin Shroud, and the Last Great Secret of Freemasonry.* Rockport, MA.: Element Publ, 1998.

Krupp, E. C. *Archaeoastronomy and the Roots of Science.* Boulder, Colo.: Westview Press, 1984.

Krupp, E. C. *Echoes of the Ancient Skies.* Oxford: Oxford Univ. Press, 1994.

Krupp, E. C. "Rambling through the skies: engraved in stone." *Sky and Telescope* vol. 89, p. 59, April, 1995.

le Carré, John. "Babes and Yarns" *Washington Post,* p. C4, August 8, 1993.

Lemaire, Andre. "The Burial Box of James, the Brother of Jesus" *Biblical Archeological Review,* Nov. 2002.

Ley, Willy. *Watchers of the Skies. An Informal History of Astronomy from Babylon to the Space Age.* NY: Viking Press, 1963.

Lincoln, Henry. *The Holy Place: The Mystery of Rennes-le-Chateau: Discovering the Eighth Wonder of the Ancient World.* New York: Arcade Publishing, 1991.

Lincoln, Henry. *Key to the Sacred Pattern. The Untold Story of Rennes-le-Chateau.* Gloucestershire: Windrush Press, 1997.

Luengo y Martinez, Jose Maria. *El Castillo de Ponferrada y los Templarios (The Castle of Ponferrada and the Templars).* Leon: Nebrija, 1980.

Mackey, Albert. *The History of Freemasonry. Its Legendary Origins.* New York: Gramercy Books, 1996.

Malville, J. M., Wendorf, F., Mazar, A. A., and Schild, R. "Megaliths and Neolithic Astronomy in Southern Egypt" *Nature* vol. 392, p. 488, 1998.

Marrs, Jim. *Rule by Secrecy: the Hidden History that Connects the Trilateral Commission, the Freemasons, and the Great Pyramids.* New York: HarperCollins, 2000.

Matthes, Walther. *Corvey und die Externsteine: Schicksal eines vorchristlichen Heiligtums in karolingischer Zeit (Corvey and the Externsteine: the Story of a pre-Christian Holy Place in the Carolingian Era).* Stuttgart: Urachhaus, 1982.

McDonagh, A. F. "Phototherapy: From ancient Egypt to the new millennium" in *Journal of Perinatology,* vol. 21, supplement 1, pp. S7–S12, 2001.

McNulty, W. Kirk. *Freemasonry—a Journey through Ritual and Symbol.* London: Thames & Hudson, 1991.

Merrifield, Jeff. *The Perfect Heretics.* Dorset: Enabler Publications, 1995.

Meyer, Marvin. *The Ancient Mysteries—A Sourcebook—Sacred Texts of the Mystery Religions of the Ancient Mediterranean World.* San Francisco: Harper & Row, 1987.

Muzzey, David. *The American Adventure I. Through the Civil War.* New York: Harper & Bros, 1927.

Neijman, M. G. E. H. *The Horse of God. Et in Arcadia Ego and the Enigma of Rennes-le-Chateau.* Belgium: Self-published CD-ROM, 1998.

Neyman, M. *The True Language of Rennes-le-Chateau.* Self-published CD-ROM: Belgium, 2000.

New Catholic Encylopedia. Washington, D.C.: Catholic University of America, 1967.

Noone, John. *The Man Behind the Iron Mask.* New York: St. Martin's Press, 1988.

North, John. *Stonehenge. A New Interpretation of Prehistoric Man and the Cosmos.* New York: Simon & Schuster (The Free Press), 1996.

Oman, C. *The History of England—from the Accession of Richard II to the Death of Richard III.* (1377-1485). New York, Greenwood Press, 1969.

Ovason, David. *The Secret Architecture of Our Nation's Capital. The Masons and the Building of Washington, D. C.* New York: HarperCollins, 2000.

Partner, Peter. *The Knights Templar and Their Myth.* Oxford: Oxford Univ. Press, 1981.

Payne, Robert. *The Dream and the Tomb. A History of the Crusades.* New York: Cooper Square Press, 2000.

Peterson, Ivars. *Newton's Clock—Chaos in the Solar System.* New York: W. H. Freeman, 1993.

Phillips, Graham. *The Search for the Grail.* London: Arrow Books, 1996.

Picknett, L., and Prince, C. *The Templar Revelation. Secret Guardians of the True Identity of Christ.* New York: Simon & Schuster, 1997.

Poe, Richard. *Black Spark, White Fire: Did African Explorers Civilize Ancient Europe?* Rocklin, CA: Prima, 1999.

Raethel, H. A. "Wavelengths of light producing photodecomposition of bilirubin in serum from a neonate with hyperbilirubinemia." In *Journal of Perinatology* vol. 87, pp. 110-114, 1975.

Richmond Times-Dispatch, April 23, 2000, pp. C1-C7.

Robinson, John. *Born in Blood: The Lost Secrets of Freemasonry.* New York: M. Evans & Co., 1989.

Robinson, John. *A Pilgrim's Path. Freemasonry and the Religious Right.* New York: M. Evans & Co., 1993.

Sakurai, Y.; Shoji, M.; Matsubara, T.; Ochiai, M.; Funabiki, T.; Urano, M.; Mizoguchi, Y.; and Fuwa, N. "Pancreatic ductal adenocarcinoma associated with Potter type II cystic disease" in *Journal of Gastroenterology* vol. 36, pp. 422-428, 2001.

"New Find Links Arthur, Tintagel" *San Jose Mercury News,* Friday, August 7, 1998.

Schmidt, Alvin J. *Fraternal Organizations.* Westport, CT: Greenwood Press, 1980.

Service, A., and Bradbery, J. *Megaliths and their Mysteries: a Guide to the Standing Stones of Europe.* New York: Macmillan, 1979.

Schonfield, Hugh. *The Jesus Party.* New York: Macmillan, 1974.

Spudis, Paul. *The Once and Future Moon.* Washington D.C.: Smithsonian Institution Press, 1996.

Stevens, Albert. *The Cyclopedia of Fraternities. A Compilation of Existing Authentic Information and the Results of Original Investigation as to the Origin, Derivation, Founders, Development, Emblems, Character, and Personnel of More Than Six Hundred Secret Societies in the United States.* New York: E. B. Treat & Co., 1907.

Stokstad, M. *Santiago de Compostela in the Age of the Great Pilgrimages.* Norman, OK: Univ. Oklahoma Press, 1978.

Sykes, H. *Mysterious Britain. Fact and Folklore.* London: Weidenfeld & Nicholson, 1993.

Taylor, Jr., L. B. *The Ghosts of Virginia. Vol. II.* Richmond, VA: Progress Printing Co., 1997.

Thiede, C., and D'Ancona M. *The Quest for the True Cross.* New York: Palgrave, 2002.

Tompkins, Peter. *Secrets of the Great Pyramid. Two Thousand Years of Adventure and Discoveries Surrounding the Mystery of the Great Pyramid of Cheops.* New York: Galahad Books, 1971.

Trochu, Francois. *Saint Bernadette Soubirous 1844-1879.* Rockford, IL: Tan Books, 1985.

Ulansey, David. *The Origins of the Mithraic Mysteries. Cosmology and Salvation in the Ancient World.* Oxford: Oxford Univ. Press, 1989.

Ulansey, David. "The Mithraic Mysteries" *Scientific American,* p. 130, Dec. 1989.

Vogel, A., Dlugos, C., Nuffer, R., and Birngruber, R. "Optical properties of human sclera, and their consequences for transscleral laser applications" in *Lasers in Surgical Medicine* vol. 11, pp. 331–340, 1991.

"Awash in Mystery: Crab Nebula's Rippling Dance" *Washington Post,* June 3, 1996, p. A3.

Waugh, Evelyn. *Brideshead Revisted.* New York: Little, Brown, 1982.

Weisweiler, Hermann. *Das Geheimnis Karls des Grossen. Astronomie in Stein: Der Aachener Dom (The Secret of Charlemagne. Astronomy in Stone: The Cathedral at Aachen).* München: Bertelsmann Verlag, 1981.

Westwood, Jennifer. *Mysterious Places: the World's Unexplained Symbolic Sites, Ancient Cities, and Lost Lands.* New York: Galahad Books, 1996.

Wetterberg, L. *Light and Biological Rhythms in Man.* New York: Pergamon Press, 1993.

Wilkinson, Richard. *The Complete Temples of Ancient Egypt.* London: Thames & Hudson, 2000.

Wilson, Ian. *The Blood and the Shroud: New Evidence that the World's Most Sacred Relic is Real.* New York: Simon & Schuster, 1998.

Wood, John E. *Sun, Moon, and Standing Stones.* London: Oxford Univ Press, 1978.

List of Illustrations

Fig. 1: Overall map of stone locations at Stonehenge

Fig. 2: Positions of the rising full moon at the summer solstice over the 18.6 year cycle

Fig. 3: Location of Stonehenge and Callanish (Isle of Lewis) in the British Isles

Fig. 4: Critical latitudes required for the astronomical alignments seen at Stonehenge and Aachen (51 degrees North) and at Rennes-le-Chateau and Santiago de Compostela (42 degrees North)

Fig. 5: Diagram of the earth's orbit, showing the inclination of the axis relative to the plane of the ecliptic

Fig. 6: Locations of Aachen and the Externsteine in Germany

Fig. 7: Overall plan of the cathedral at Aachen, seen from above (after Weisweiler, 1981)

Fig. 8: Map of the Aachen area, showing alignments of medieval structures along the sunrise line at the summer solstice (after Weisweiler, 1981)

Fig. 9: Location of Rennes-le-Chateau in France

Fig. 10: Pentagonal arrangement of mountain peaks and structures in the area of Rennes-le-Chateau

Fig. 11: Astronomical alignments of churches in the area of Rennes-le-Chateau

Fig. 12: Pentagonal geometry in *The Assumption of the Virgin* by Nicholas Poussin

Fig. 13: First Degree Tracing Board depicting the astronomical symbolism of Freemasonry

Fig. 14: Location of Santiago de Compostela in Spain

Fig. 15: Overall view of the location of the cathedral in Santiago de Compostela

Fig. 16: Artwork typically found in a Mithraic shrine

About the Author

JOHN YOUNG IS A PROFESSOR OF histology and cell biology at Howard University. He got his Ph.D. in Anatomy from UCLA, but has a variety of non-career interests, including history, astronomy, archeology, and languages; he speaks Spanish, Russian, and German, all of which helped in reading non-translated material used to research this book. This is his fifth book; previous books were two popular books on science and two translations of neuroscience books from the Russian. He lives in Vienna, Virginia with his wife and two sons.

229

Index

ALSO FROM FAIR WINDS PRESS

The Hiram Key
Pharaohs, Freemasonry, and the Discovery of the Secret Scrolls of Jesus
Christopher Knight and Robert Lomas

The Hiram Key is a book that will shake the Christian world to its very roots. When Christopher Knight and Robert Lomas, both Masons, set out to find the origins of Freemasonry they had no idea that they would find themselves unraveling the true story of Jesus Christ and the original Jerusalem Church. As a radically new picture of Jesus started to emerge, the authors came to the controversial conclusion that the key rituals of modern Freemasonry were practiced by the sect as a means of initiation into their community.

ISBN: 1-931412-75-8
$18.95
Paperback; 400 pages
Available wherever books
are sold

The Second Messiah
Templars, the Turin Shroud, and the Great Secret of Freemasonry
Christopher Knight and Robert Lomas

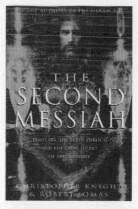

Is the Shroud of Turin genuine?

For almost seven and a half centuries, a piece of cloth was venerated because it bore the image of the crucified Christ, but results of carbon dating have shown that the fabric could not have pre-dated 1260. Now new evidence conclusively proves that it is not a fake...yet neither is it the image of Jesus Christ.

In the follow-up to their ground-breaking first book, *The Hiram Key*, Christopher Knight and Robert Lomas continue their research into the mysteries of Freemasonry and the true historical Jesus, and uncover the precise time and place of the shroud's creation.

ISBN: 1-931412-76-6
$18.95
Paperback; 272 pages
Available wherever books
are sold

The answer to the great mystery of the Shroud of Turin will surprise and astonish as the authors unlock the secrets of abandoned Freemason rituals and the man who would be called the Second Messiah!

238

ALSO FROM FAIR WINDS PRESS

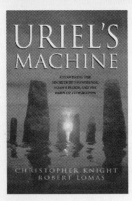

ISBN: 1-931412-74-X
$18.95
Paperback; 480 pages
Available wherever books
are sold

Uriel's Machine

Uncovering the Secrets of Stonehenge, Noah's Flood, and the Dawn of Civilization
Christopher Knight and Robert Lomas

Noah's Flood Was Real—With Worldwide Consequences!

Uriel's Machine presents evidence that:
• There was a single global language on Earth
• A single female was a common ancestor to all living humans
• Angels bred with human women to create The Watchers, giant half-human beings
• The oral tradition of Freemasonry records real events

A fascinating study of humankind's past, present, and future, *Uriel's Machine* proves the world was indeed flooded, but survived wholly due to the ancient Europeans, their heavenly knowledge, and one remarkable machine.

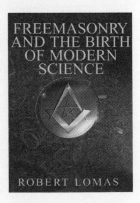

ISBN: 1-931412-74-X
$18.95
Paperback; 480 pages
Available wherever books
are sold

Freemasonry and the Birth of Modern Science
Robert Lomas

In 1660, within a few months of the restoration of Charles II, a group of twelve men met in London to set up a society to study the mechanisms of nature. At a time when superstition and magic governed reason, the repressive dogma of Christian belief silenced many, and where post-war loyalties ruined careers, these men forbade the discussion of religion and politics at their meetings. The Royal Society was born and with it modern, experimental science.

Freemasonry and the Birth of Modern Science will make you reassess many of the key events of this period and will show how Freemasonry was the guiding force behind the birth of modern science, under the cover of the Royal Society.

Robert Lomas became a Freemason in 1986, and was a popular lecturer on Masonic history before co-authoring the international bestsellers, *The Hiram Key*, *The Second Messiah*, and *Uriel's Machine*. He currently lectures in Information Systems at Bradford University School of Management.

ALSO FROM FAIR WINDS PRESS

Bloodline of the Holy Grail
The Hidden Lineage of Jesus Revealed
Laurence Gardner

From royal and suppressed archives comes documented proof of the heritage of Jesus in the West and the long awaited discovery of the Holy Grail. In fulfilling this time-honoured quest, penetrating new light is cast upon the Grail Code of Service and the venerated feminine element, upheld in chivalry but forsaken by the Church in order to forge a male dominated society.

Featuring all the charm and adventure of Arthurian romance, coupled with enthralling Rosicrucian and Templar disclosures, this extraordinary work has a cutting edge of intrigue which removes the established blanket of enigma to expose one of the greatest conspiracies ever told.

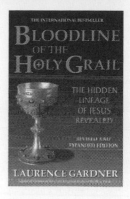

ISBN 1-931412-92-8
$18.95
Paperback/464 pages
16-page color insert
Available wherever books are sold

Genesis of the Grail Kings
The Explosive Story of Genetic Cloning and the Ancient Bloodline of Jesus
Laurence Gardner

From beneath the windswept sands of ancient Mesopotamia comes the documented legacy of the creation chamber of the heavenly Anunnaki. Here is the story of the clinical cloning of Adam and Eve, which predates Bible scripture by more than 2,000 years.

From cuneiform texts, cylinder seals, and suppressed archives, best-selling historian and distinguished genealogist Laurence Gardner tells the ultimate story of the alchemical bloodline of the Holy Grail.

"A truly groundbreaking piece of work. The complicated and vast material is handled superbly. Absolutely mind-blowing!"
Science of Thought Review

ISBN 1-931412-93-6
$18.95
Paperback/386 pages
16-page color insert
Available wherever books are sold

ALSO FROM FAIR WINDS PRESS

Realm of the Ring Lords
The Myth and Magic of the Grail Quest
Laurence Gardner

ISBN: 1-931412-14-6
$18.95
Paperback; 432 pages
Available wherever books
are sold

The truth behind the time-honored quests for the Ring and
the Grail!

The magical history of the Ring Lords, alluded to in
J.R.R. Tolkien's *The Lord of the Rings*, has been largely con-
signed to legend and half-remembered battles between good
and evil. Shrouded in supernatural enigma, its legacy lives on
in fascinating tales of fairies, elves, witches, and vampires.

Why do we sense deeper truths behind the mysteries of
the Ring and the Grail? Why have their common enchant-
ments been distorted and hidden?

The ancient guardians of our culture have never been
featured positively in academic teachings. Instead, their reality
was quashed from the earliest days of Inquisitional suppression
and the literal diminution of their figures caused a parallel
diminishing of their history. In truth, however, the sovereign
legacy of our culture comes from a place and time that might
just as well be called Middle-earth as by any other name.
It lingers beyond the twilight portal in the long distant realm
of the Ring Lords.